asx

MY LIFE

TROTSKY AT EIGHTEEN, WHEN HIS CAREER AS A
REVOLUTIONARY BEGAN

LEON TROTSKY

MY LIFE

An Attempt at an Autobiography

1930

CHARLES SCRIBNER'S SONS

NEW YORK

FOREWORD

OUR times again are rich in memoirs, perhaps richer than ever before. It is because there is much to tell. The more dramatic and rich in change the epoch, the more intense the interest in current history. The art of landscape-painting could never have been born in the Sahara. The "crossing" of two epochs, as at present, gives rise to a desire to look back at yesterday, already far away, through the eyes of its active participants. That is the reason for the enormous growth in the literature of reminiscence since the days of the last war. Perhaps it will justify the present volume as well.

The very fact of its coming into the world is due to the pause in the author's active political life. One of the unforeseen, though not accidental, stops in my life has proved to be Constantinople. Here I am camping—but not for the first time—and patiently waiting for what is to follow. The life of a revolutionary would be quite impossible without a certain amount of "fatalism." In one way or another, the Constantinople interval has proved the most appropriate moment for me to look back before circumstances allow me to move forward.

At first I wrote cursory autobiographical sketches for the newspapers, and thought I would let it go at that. And here I would like to say that, from my refuge, I was unable to watch the form in which those sketches reached the public. But every work has its own logic. I did not get into my stride until I had nearly finished those articles. Then I decided to write a book. I applied a different and infinitely broader scale, and carried out the whole work anew. The only point in common between the original newspaper articles and this book is that both discuss the same subject. In everything else they are two different products.

I have dealt in especial detail with the second period of the Soviet revolution, the beginning of which coincided with Lenin's illness and the opening of the campaign against "Trotskyism." The struggle of the epigones for power, as I shall try to prove, was not merely a struggle of personalities; it represented a new political chapter—the reaction against October, and the preparation of the Thermidor. From this the answer to the question

v

that I have so often been asked—"How did you lose power?"—follows naturally.

An autobiography of a revolutionary politician must inevitably touch on a whole series of theoretical questions connected with the social development of Russia, and in part with humanity as a whole, but especially with those critical periods that are called revolutions. Of course I have not been able in these pages to examine complicated theoretical problems critically in their essence. The so-called theory of permanent revolution, which played so large a rôle in my personal life, and, what is more important, is acquiring such poignant reality in the countries of the East, runs through this book as a remote leit-motif. If this does not satisfy the reader, I can say that the consideration of the problem of revolution in its essence will constitute a separate book, in which I shall attempt to give form to the principal theoretical conclusions of the experiences of the last decades.

As many people pass through the pages of my book, portrayed not always in the light that they would have chosen for themselves or for their parties, many of them will find my account lacking the necessary detachment. Even extracts that have been published in the newspapers have elicited certain denials. That is inevitable. One has no doubt that even if I had succeeded in making my autobiography a mere daguerreotype of my life—which I never intended it to be—it would nevertheless have called forth echoes of the discussion started at the time by the collisions described in the book. This book is not a dispassionate photograph of my life, however, but a component part of it. In these pages, I continue the struggle to which my whole life is devoted. Describing, I also characterize and evaluate; narrating, I also defend myself, and more often attack. It seems to me that this is the only method of making an autobiography objective in a higher sense, that is, of making it the most adequate expression of personality, conditions, and epoch.

Objectivity is not the pretended indifference with which confirmed hypocrisy, in speaking of friends and enemies, suggests indirectly to the reader what it finds inconvenient to state directly. Objectivity of this sort is nothing but a conventional trick. I do not need it. Since I have submitted to the necessity of writing about myself—nobody has as yet succeeded in writing an autobiography without writing about himself—I can have no reason to hide my sympathies or antipathies, my loves or my hates.

This is a book of polemics. It reflects the dynamics of that social life which is built entirely on contradictions. The impertinence of the schoolboy toward his master; the pin-pricks of envy in the drawing-room, veiled by courtesies; the constant competition of commerce; the frenzied rivalry in all branches of pure and applied science, of art, and sport; the parliamentary clashes that reveal the deep opposition of interests; the furious struggle that goes on every day in the newspapers; the strikes of the workers; the shooting down of participants in demonstrations; the packages of explosives that civilized neighbors send each other through the air; the fiery tongues of civil war, almost never extinguished on our planet—all these are the forms of social "polemics," ranging from those that are usual, constant and normal, almost unnoticed despite their intensity, to those of war and revolution that are extraordinary, explosive and volcanic. Such is our epoch. We have all grown up with it. We breathe it and live by it. How can we help being polemical if we want to be true to our period in the mode of the day?

But there is another and more elementary criterion, one that relates to plain conscientiousness in stating facts. Just as the most bitter revolutionary struggle must take account of time and place, the most polemical work must observe the proportions that exist between objects and men. I hope that I have observed this demand not only in its entirety, but also in its particulars.

In certain cases—although these are not very numerous— I relate long-ago conversations in dialogue form. No one will demand a verbatim report of conversations repeated many years after. Nor do I claim such accuracy. Some of these dialogues have rather a symbolic character. Every one, however, has had moments in his life when some particular conversation has impressed itself indelibly on his memory. One usually repeats that sort of conversation to one's personal or political friends; thanks to this, they become fixed in one's memory. I am thinking primarily, of course, of all conversations of a political nature.

I may state here that I am accustomed to trust to my memory. Its testimony has been subjected to verification by fact more than once, and it has stood the test perfectly. But a reservation is necessary. If my topographic memory, not to mention my musical one, is very weak, and my visual memory and my linguistic memory fairly mediocre, still my memory of ideas is considerably above the average. And, moreover, in this book ideas, their evolution, and the struggle of men for these ideas, have the most important place.

It is true that memory is not an automatic reckoner. Above all, it is never disinterested. Not infrequently it expels or drives into a dark corner episodes not convenient to the vital instinct that controls it—usually ambition. But this is a matter for "psychoanalytic" criticism, which is sometimes very ingenious and instructive, but more often capricious and arbitrary.

Needless to say, I have persistently checked my memory by documentary evidence. Difficult as the conditions of my work have been, in the business of making inquiries in libraries or searching out archives I have been able to verify all the more important facts and dates that were needed.

Beginning with 1897, I have waged the fight chiefly with a pen in my hand. Thus the events of my life have left an almost uninterrupted trail in print over a period of thirty-two years. The factional struggle in the party, which began in 1903, has been rich in personal episodes. My opponents, like myself, have not withheld blows. All of them have left their scars in print. Since the October revolution, the history of the revolutionary movement has held an important place in the research work of young Soviet scholars and of entire institutions. Everything of interest is sought out in the archives of the revolution and of the Czarist police department and published with detailed factual commentaries. In the first years, when there was as yet no need of disguising anything, this work was carried on most conscientiously. The "works" of Lenin and some of mine were issued by the State Publishing House, with notes that took up dozens of pages in each volume and contained invaluable factual material concerning both the activities of the authors and the events of the corresponding period. All this of course facilitated my work, helping me to fix the correct chronological pattern and to avoid errors of fact, at least the most serious ones.

I cannot deny that my life has not followed quite the ordinary course. The reasons for that are inherent in the conditions of the time, rather than in me. Of course certain personal traits were also necessary for the work, good or bad, that I performed. But under other historical conditions, these personal peculiarities might have remained completely dormant, as is true of so many propensities and passions on which the social environment makes no demands. On the other hand, other qualities to-day crowded out or suppressed might have come to the fore. Above the subjective there rises the objective, and in the final reckoning it is the objective that decides.

My intellectual and active life, which began when I was about seventeen or eighteen years old, has been one of constant struggle for definite ideas. In my personal life there were no events deserving public attention in themselves. All the more or less unusual episodes in my life are bound up with the revolutionary struggle, and derive their significance from it. This alone justifies the appearance of my autobiography. But from this same source flow many difficulties for the author. The facts of my personal life have proved to be so closely interwoven with the texture of historical events that it has been difficult to separate them. This book, moreover, is not altogether an historical work. Events are treated here not according to their objective significance, but according to the way in which they are connected with the facts of my personal life. It is quite natural, then, that the accounts of specific events and of entire periods lack the proportion that would be demanded of them if this book were an historical work. I had to grope for the dividing line between autobiography and the history of the revolution. Without allowing the story of my life to become lost in an historical treatise, it was necessary at the same time to give the reader a base of the facts of the social development. In doing this, I assumed that the main outlines of the great events were known to him, and that all his memory needed was a brief reminder of historical facts and their sequence.

By the time this book is published, I shall have reached my fiftieth birthday. The date coincides with that of the October revolution. Mystics and Pythagoreans may draw from this whatever conclusions they like. I myself noticed this odd coincidence only three years after the October uprising. Until I was nine years old I lived in a remote little village. For eight years I studied at school. I was arrested for the first time a year after I left school. For universities, like many others of my time, I had prison, Siberia, and foreign exile. In the Czar's prisons I served four years in two periods. In the Czarist exile I spent about two years the first time, a few weeks the second. I escaped from Siberia twice. As a foreign émigré, I lived for about twelve years altogether in various European countries and in America— two years before the revolution of 1905, and nearly ten years after its defeat. In 1915, during the war, I was sentenced in my absence to imprisonment in Hohenzollern Germany; the next year I was expelled from France and Spain, and after a brief stay in the Madrid prison, and a month in Cadiz under the surveillance of the police, I was deported to America. I was there when the February revolution broke out. On my way from New York I was arrested by the British in March, 1917, and detained for a month in a concentration camp in Canada. I took part in the revolutions of 1905 and 1917, and I was the chairman of the St. Petersburg Soviet of delegates in 1905, and again in 1917. I took an intimate part in the October revolution, and was a member of the Soviet government. As the People's Commissary for foreign affairs, I conducted peace negotiations at Brest-Litovsk with the delegates of Germany, Austria-Hungary, Turkey and Bulgaria. As People's Commissary for military and naval affairs, I devoted about five years to organizing the Red army and restoring the Red navy. During the year 1920 I added to that the direction of the country's disorganized railway system.

The main content of my life, however, except for the years of the civil war, has been party and literary activity. In 1923 the State Publishing House began the publication of my collected works. It succeeded in bringing out thirteen volumes, not counting the previously published five volumes on military subjects. Publication was discontinued in 1927, when the persecution of "Trotskyism" became especially intense.

In January, 1928, I was sent into exile by the present Soviet government; I spent a year on the Chinese frontier; in February, 1929, I was deported to Turkey, and I am now writing these lines from Constantinople.

Even in this condensed synopsis, the outward course of my life could hardly be called monotonous. On the contrary, counting the number of turns, surprises, sharp conflicts, ups and downs, one might say that my life was rather full of "adventures." But I must say that, by natural inclination, I have nothing in common with seekers after adventure. I am rather pedantic and conservative in my habits. I like and appreciate discipline and system. Not to provide a paradox, but because it is a fact, I must add that I cannot endure disorder or destruction. I was always an accurate and diligent schoolboy, and I have preserved these two qualities all my life. In the years of the civil war, when I covered by train a distance equal to several times round the earth, I was greatly pleased to see each new fence constructed of freshly cut pine boards. Lenin, who knew this passion of mine, often twitted me about it in a friendly way. A well-written book in which one can find new ideas, and a good pen with which to communicate one's own ideas to others, for me have always been and are to-day the most valuable and intimate products of culture. The desire for study has never left me, and many times in my life I felt that the revolution was interfering with my systematic work. Yet almost a third of a century of my conscious life was entirely filled with revolutionary struggle. And if I had to live it over again, I would unhesitatingly take the same path.

I am obliged to write these lines as an émigré—for the third time—while my closest friends are filling the places of exile and the prisons of that Soviet republic in whose creating they took so decisive a part. Some of them are vacillating, withdrawing, bowing before the enemy. Some are doing it because they are morally exhausted; others because they can find no other way out of the maze of circumstances; and still others because of the pressure of material reprisals. I had already lived through two instances of such mass desertion of the banner: after the collapse of the revolution of 1905, and at the beginning of the World War. Thus I know well enough, from my own experience, the historical ebb and flow. They are governed by their own laws. Mere impatience will not expedite their change. I have grown accustomed to viewing the historical perspective not from the standpoint of my personal fate. To understand the causal sequence of events and to find somewhere in the sequence one's own place —that is the first duty of a revolutionary. And at the same time, it is the greatest personal satisfaction possible for a man who does not limit his tasks to the present day.

L. TROTSKY.

PRINKIPO, 1929.

CONTENTS

CONTENTS

MY LIFE

CHAPTER I

YANOVKA

CHILDHOOD is looked upon as the happiest time of life. Is that always true? No, only a few have a happy childhood. The idealization of childhood originated in the old literature of the privileged. A secure, affluent, and unclouded childhood, spent in a home of inherited wealth and culture, a childhood of affection and play, brings back to one memories of a sunny meadow at the beginning of the road of life. The grandees of literature, or the plebeians who glorify the grandees, have canonized this purely aristocratic view of childhood. But the majority of the people, if it looks back at all, sees, on the contrary, a childhood of darkness, hunger and dependence. Life strikes the weak—and who is weaker than a child?

My childhood was not one of hunger and cold. My family had already achieved a competence at the time of my birth. But it was the stern competence of people still rising from poverty and having no desire to stop half-way. Every muscle was strained, every thought set on work and savings. Such a domestic routine left but a modest place for the children. We knew no need, but neither did we know the generosities of life—its caresses. My childhood does not appear to me like a sunny meadow, as it does to the small minority; neither does it appear like a dark cave of hunger, violence and misery, as it does to the majority. Mine was the grayish childhood of a lower-middle-class family, spent in a village in an obscure corner where nature is wide, and manners, views and interests are pinched and narrow.

The spiritual atmosphere which surrounded my early years and that in which I passed my later, conscious life are two different worlds, divided not only in time and space by decades and by far countries, but by the mountain chains of great events and by those inner landslides which are less obvious but are

I

fully as important to one's individuality. When I first began
to draft these memoirs, it often seemed to me as if I were not
writing of my own childhood but of a long-past journey into a
distant land. I even attempted to write my story in the third
person, but this conventional form all too easily smacks of fic-
tion, which is something that I should want to avoid at all
costs.

In spite of the contradiction between these two worlds, the
unity of the personality passes through hidden channels from
one world into the other. This, generally speaking, accounts
for the interest that people take in the biographies and auto-
biographies of those who, for one reason or another, have occupied a somewhat more spacious place in the life of society.
I shall therefore try to tell the story of my childhood in some
detail,—without anticipating and predetermining the future,
that is, without selecting the facts to suit preconceived generalities—simply narrating what occurred as it is preserved
in my memory.

At times it has seemed to me that I can remember suckling
at my mother's breast; probably I apply to myself only what
I have seen in the younger children. I have a dim recollection
of a scene under an apple-tree in the garden which took place
when I was a year and a half old, but that memory too is
doubtful. More securely do I remember another event: I am
with my mother in Bobrinetz, visiting the Z. family, where
there is a little girl of two or three. I am the bridegroom, the
little girl is the bride. The children are playing on the painted
floor of the parlor; the little girl fades away; the little boy is
standing dazed and petrified beside a chest of drawers. His
mother and the hostess come in. His mother looks at the boy,
then at the puddle beside him, and then at the boy again, shakes
her head reproachfully and says: "Aren't you ashamed of yourself?" The boy looks at his mother, at himself, and at the puddle, as if it all had nothing whatever to do with him.

"Never mind," the hostess says, "the children have played
too long."

The little boy feels neither shame nor repentance. How old
was he then? About two years, possibly three.

It was about this time that I ran into a poisonous snake

while walking in the garden with my nurse. "Look, Lyova!"*
she cried, pointing to a bright object in the grass. "Here is a
snuff-box buried in the ground!" My nurse took a stick and
began to dig it out. She herself was not more than sixteen
years old. The snuff-box uncoiled itself, stretched into a snake,
and, hissing, began to crawl in the grass. "Ai! Ai!" screamed
my nurse, and, catching me by the hand, ran quickly. It was
hard for me to move my legs fast enough. Choking with excitement, I told afterward of our finding in the grass a snuff-
box which turned into a snake.

I remember another early scene that took place in our main
kitchen. Neither my father nor my mother is at home. The
cook and the maid and their guests are there. My older
brother, Alexander, who is at home for the holidays, is also
buzzing about, standing on a wooden shovel, as if on a pair
of stilts, and dancing on it across the earthen floor. I beg
my brother to let me have the shovel, and try to climb up on it,
but I fall down and cry. My brother picks me up, kisses me,
and carries me out of the kitchen in his arms.

I must have been about four years old when some one put
me on the back of a big gray mare as gentle as a sheep, with
neither bridle nor saddle, only a rope halter. I spread my legs
wide apart and held on to the mane with both hands. The
mare quietly took me to a pear-tree and walked under a branch,
which caught me across the middle. Not realizing what the
matter was, I slid over the mare's rump, and hit the grass. I
was not hurt, only puzzled.

I had almost no ready-made toys in my childhood. Once,
however, my mother brought me a cardboard horse and a ball
from Kharkoff. My younger sister and I played with dolls
which we made ourselves. Once Aunt Fenya and Aunt Raisa,
my father's sisters, made some rag dolls for us and Aunt
Fenya marked their eyes, noses and mouths with a pencil. The
dolls seemed remarkable to me; I can remember them to this
day. One winter evening our mechanic, Ivan Vasilyevich, cut

* Trotsky's full and original name was Lev Davydovich Bronstein, his father's
name being Davyd Leontiyevich Bronstein. "Lyova" is one of the many sim-
ilar diminutives of Lev, which literally means "Lion." In English and French
usage, Trotsky has become known as Leon, in German as Leo. In ensuing pages
the reader will frequently find him referred to as Lev Davydovich, and often in
quotations from his wife's journal simply as L. D.—*Translator.*

a little railway-car with wheels and windows out of card-board and pasted it together. My older brother, at home for Christmas, instantly announced that he could make a car too, in no time. He began by pulling my car to pieces; then he armed himself with a ruler, pencil and scissors, and drew for a long time. But when he cut out what he had drawn, there was no railway-car.

Our relatives and friends, when going to town, would some-times ask what I wanted from Elizavetgrad or Nikolayev. My eyes would shine. What should I ask for? They would come to my help. One would suggest a toy horse, another books, another colored crayons, another a pair of skates. "I want half-Halifax skates!" I would cry, having heard this expres-sion from my brother. But they would forget their promises as soon as they had crossed the threshold. I lived in hope for several weeks, and then suffered a long disappointment.

A bee sits on a sunflower in the garden. Because bees sting and must be handled with care, I pick up a burdock leaf and with it seize the bee between two fingers. I am suddenly pierced by an unendurable pain. I run screaming across the yard to the machine-shop, where Ivan Vasilyevich pulls out the sting and smears a healing liquid on my finger.

Ivan Vasilyevich had a jar full of sunflower-oil in which tarantulas were floating. This was considered the best cure for stings. Victor Ghertopanov and I together used to catch these tarantulas. To do this, we would fasten a piece of wax to a thread and drop it into one of their burrows. The tarantula would seize the wax in its claws and stick tight. We then had only to draw it out and catch it in an empty match-box. These tarantula hunts, however, must have belonged to a later period.

I remember a conversation on a long winter evening during which my elders discussed over their tea when it was that Ya-novka had been bought, how old such and such a child was at the time, and when Ivan Vasilyevich had come to work for us. My mother speaks, glancing slyly at me: "We brought Lyova here from the farm all ready-made." I try to reason that out for myself, and finally say aloud: "Then I was born on the farm?" "No," they answer me, "you were born here at Yanovka."

"Then why did Mother say that you brought me here ready-made?"

"Mother was just joking!"

But I am not satisfied, and I think it is a queer joke. I hold my peace, however, for I notice that particular smile that I never can bear on the faces of the older initiates. It is from these recollections exchanged at leisure over our winter tea that a certain chronology emerges: I was born on the 26th of October. My parents must have moved from the little farm to Yanovka either in the spring or summer of 1879.

The year of my birth was the year of the first dynamite assaults against Czarism. The recently formed terrorist party, the "People's Will," had on August 26th, 1879, two months before my appearance in the world, pronounced the death sentence on Alexander II. And on November 19th an attempt was made to dynamite the Czar's train. The ominous struggle which led to the assassination of Alexander II on March 1st, 1881, and at the same time resulted in the annihilation of the "People's Will," was just beginning.

The Russo-Turkish War had ended the year before. In August, 1879, Bismarck laid the foundations of the Austro-Germanic Alliance. In this year Zola brought out his novel, *Nana,* in which the future originator of the Entente, then only the Prince of Wales, was introduced as a refined connoisseur of musical-comedy stars. The wind of reaction which had risen after the Franco-Prussian War and the fall of the Paris Commune was still blowing strongly through the politics of Europe. Social Democracy in Germany had already fallen under Bismarck's discriminatory legislation. In 1879 Victor Hugo and Louis Blanc demanded in the French Chamber of Deputies an amnesty for the Communards.

But neither the echoes of parliamentary debates nor those of diplomatic events, not even those of the explosions of dynamite, could be heard in the village of Yanovka where I first saw the light, and where I spent the first nine years of my life. On the boundless steppes of Kherson and of all South Russia was a kingdom of wheat and sheep, living by laws all its own. It was firmly guarded against the invasion of politics by its great open spaces and the absence of roads. Only the numerous barrows on the steppes remained as landmarks of the great migration of nations.

My father was a farmer, first on a small scale and later on

a larger one. As a little boy, he had left with his parents the Jewish town in the Province of Poltava, where he had been born, when they went to seek their fortune on the free steppes of the South. There were at that time about forty Jewish agricultural colonies in the provinces of Kherson and Ekaterinoslav, with a total population of about 25,000 souls. The Jewish farmers were on an equal footing with the other peasants not only as regards their legal rights (until 1881), but also as regards their property. By indefatigable, cruel toil that spared neither himself nor others, and by hoarding every penny, my father rose in the world.

The registration book was not kept very accurately in the colony of Gromokley, and many entries were made after the date of the events recorded. When the time came for me to enter high school, it appeared that I was still too young for admission. The year of my birth was then changed in the birth certificate from 1879 to 1878; so I always had two records, my official age and the one observed by my family.

For the first nine years of my life I hardly stuck my nose outside my native village. Its name, Yanovka, came from the name of the landlord Yanovsky, from whom the estate had been bought. The old proprietor, Yanovsky, had risen from the ranks to a Colonelcy, had won the favor of the powers that be in the reign of Alexander II, and had been given the choice of one thousand acres of land on the uninhabited steppes of the province of Kherson. He built himself a mud hut thatched with straw, and equally crude farm-buildings. But his farming did not prosper, and after the Colonel's death his family moved to Poltava. My father bought over two hundred and fifty acres of land from Yanovsky and leased about four hundred more. I remember the Colonel's widow well. She was a dried-up little old woman who came once or twice a year to collect her rent from us and to see that everything was in order. We would send our spring wagon to meet her at the station and bring a chair to the front steps to make it easier for her to alight. The phaeton made its appearance at my father's later, after he had acquired driving stallions. The Colonel's widow would be served chicken bouillon and soft-boiled eggs. Walking with my sister in the garden, she would scratch the resin from the fence-posts with her shrivelled fingers, and assure her that it was the most delicate sweetmeat in the world.

YANOVKA

My father's crops increased, as did the herds of cattle and horses. There was even an attempt to keep Merino sheep, but the venture was unsuccessful; on the other hand there were plenty of pigs. They wandered freely all over the place, rooted everywhere, and completely destroyed the garden. The estate was managed with care, but in an old-fashioned way. One measured profit or loss with the eye. For that very reason, it would have been difficult to fix the extent of father's fortune. All of his substance was always either in the ground, or in the crop above, or in the stocks on hand, which were either in bins or on their way to a port. Sometimes in the midst of tea or supper my father would suddenly exclaim: "Come, write this down! I have received thirteen hundred roubles from the commission merchant. I gave the Colonel's widow six hundred, and four hundred to Dembovsky. Put down, too, that I gave Theodosia Antonovna one hundred roubles when I was in Elizavetgrad last spring." That is about the way he kept his books. Nevertheless, my father slowly but obstinately kept climbing upward.

We lived in the little mud house that the Colonel had built. The straw roof harbored countless sparrows' nests under the eaves. The walls on the outside were seamed with deep cracks which were a breeding-place for adders. Sometimes these adders were mistaken for poisonous snakes, and boiling water from the samovar went into the cracks, but to no avail. The low ceilings leaked during a heavy rain, especially in the hall, and pots and basins would be placed on the dirt floor to catch the water. The rooms were small, the windows dim; the floors in the two bedrooms and the nursery were of clay, and bred fleas. The dining-room boasted a wooden floor which was rubbed once a week with yellow sand. But the floor in the main room, which was solemnly named the parlor, though only about eight paces long, was painted. The Colonel's widow stayed here.

Yellow acacias, red and white roses, and in summer a climbing vine, grew around the house. The courtyard was not fenced in at all. A big mud house with a tile roof, which my father had built, contained the machine-shop, the main kitchen, and the servants' quarters. Next to it stood the "little" wooden barn and beyond that the "big" barn. Beyond that again came

7

the "new" barn. All were thatched with reeds. The barns were raised upon stones so that water trickling under them would not mould the grain. In hot or cold weather the dogs, pigs and chickens would take refuge under the barns. There the hens found a quiet place to lay their eggs. I used to fetch out the eggs, crawling in among the stones on my stomach; the space was too small for a grown person to squeeze into. Storks would nest every year on the roof of the "big" barn. They would raise their red bills to heaven as they swallowed adders and frogs—a terrible sight! Their bodies would wriggle from their bills downward, and it looked as if the snake were eating the stork from the inside.

The barns, divided into bins, held fresh-smelling wheat, rough-prickly barley, smooth, almost liquid flaxseed, the blue-black beads of the winter rape, and light, slender oats. When the children played at hide-and-seek, they were allowed, on occasions when there were special guests, to hide in the barns. Crawling over one of the partitions into a bin, I would scramble up the mound of wheat and slip down on the other side. My arms would be buried to the elbows and my legs to the knees in the sliding mass of wheat, and my shirt and shoes, too often torn, would be filled with grain; the door of the barn would be shut, and some one, for the sake of appearances, would hang a padlock on the outside without snapping it, according to the rules of the game. I would be lying in the cool barn, buried in grain, breathing its dust, and listening to Senya V. or Senya J. or Senya S. or my sister Liza or some one else running about the courtyard, finding the others but not finding me, submerged in the winter-wheat.

The stable, the cowshed, the pigsty, and the chicken-house all stood on the other side of our dwelling. These were all made of mud and straw and twigs, somehow stuck together with clay. The tall well-sweep rose toward heaven about a hundred yards from the house. Beyond the well lay the pond that watered the gardens of the peasants. The spring freshets carried the dam away every year, and it had to be rebuilt with earth and manure and straw. On the hill above the pond stood the mill—a wooden shed which sheltered a ten-horse-power steam-engine and two millstones. Here, during the first years of my childhood, my mother spent the greater part of her working hours. The mill worked not only for our own estate but for the whole neighborhood as well. The peasants brought their grain in from ten and fifteen miles around and paid a tenth measure for the grinding. In hot weather, on the eve of the threshing season, the mill worked day and night, and when I had learned to count and write, I used to weigh the peasants' grain and calculate the price of the grinding. When the harvest was over the mill was closed and the engine went out to thresh. Later a stationary engine was installed in a new stone and tile building. Our old mud house, too, was replaced by a large brick one with a tin roof. But all this happened when I had already reached my seventeenth year. During my last summer holidays I used to calculate the distance between the windows, and the sizes of the doors for our new house, but I never could make the lines meet. On my next visit to the country I saw the stone foundation being built. I never lived in the house itself. It is now used as a Soviet school.

The peasants often used to wait at the mill for weeks to have their grain ground. Those who lived near by would leave their sacks in line and go home. Those who came from far away lived in their wagons, and in rainy weather slept in the mill. One of these peasants once lost a bridle. Some one had seen a boy roving about near a certain horse. The peasants rushed to his father's wagon and looked under the straw; there lay the bridle! The boy's father, a gloomy, bearded peasant, faced the East and crossed himself, swearing that the damned little rascal, the scoundrelly jailbird, had taken it unknown to himself, and that he would take the hide off him for it. But no one believed the father. So the peasant caught his son and began beating him with the stolen bridle. I watched this scene from behind the backs of the grown-ups. The boy screamed and swore he would never steal again. The peasants stood about, gloomily looking on, entirely indifferent to the cries of the boy. They smoked their cigarettes and muttered in their beards that the father was speciously beating his son only for appearances' sake, and that he himself should be flogged too.

Beyond the barns and the sheds for animals, extended two enormous sheds hundreds of feet long, one of reeds and the other of straw, built in the shape of a gabled roof resting directly on the ground, without walls. The fresh grain was piled under these sheds, and here the men worked with winnowers and sieves in rainy or windy weather. Beyond the sheds lay the threshing-floor. Across a ravine lay the cowpen, its walls built entirely of dry manure.

All my childish life is connected with the Colonel's mud house and the old sofa in the dining-room there. This sofa was veneered to look like red wood, and on it I sat for tea, for dinner and for supper. Here I played dolls with my sister, and here I would later read. The cover was torn in two places. The smaller hole was near the chair where Ivan Vasilyevich sat, the larger where I sat, next to my father. "This sofa should have a new cover," Ivan Vasilyevich used to say.

"It should have had one long ago," my mother would reply. "We haven't covered it since the year the Czar was killed."

"But you know," my father would justify himself, "when one gets to that damned city, one runs here and there, the cab costs money, one is thinking all the time about how to get back quickly to the farm, and forgets all about what one came to buy."

A rough, unpainted rafter stretched across the low ceiling of the dining-room, and on this the most varied objects found their resting-place: plates of provisions for safekeeping from the cat, nails, string, books, ink-bottles stoppered with paper, a penholder with an old rusty pen. There was no superfluity of pens at Yanovka. There were times when I made a pen for myself out of wood with the help of a table-knife, for copying horses out of old numbers of the illustrated magazine, *Field*. Up under the ceiling, where the chimney went out, lived the cat. There she raised her kittens, bravely jumping down with them in her teeth when it grew too hot up there. If a guest were tall he always hit the rafter with his head when he rose from the table, so that we had acquired the habit of pointing upward and saying: "Mind your head!"

The most striking object in the parlor was an old spinet that occupied at least a quarter of the room. I can remember when it appeared. The wife of a bankrupt landowner, who lived some fifteen miles away, moved into town and sold her household goods. From her we bought the sofa, three bentwood chairs, and the old tumble-down spinet with broken strings that had been standing in an outhouse for years. My father paid sixteen roubles for it and brought it to Yanovka on a cart. A pair of dead mice were found in it when it was overhauled in the machine-shop. The shop was occupied by the spinet for several winter weeks. Ivan Vasilyevich cleaned it, glued it, polished it, found new strings, and put them in and tuned them. All the keys were replaced, and the voice of the spinet resounded in the parlor. It was feeble, but irresistible. Ivan Vasilyevich transferred his magic fingers from the stops of his accordion to the keys of the spinet, and played the Kamarinskaya, polkas, and "Mein Lieber Augustine." My oldest sister began to take music lessons. My oldest brother had taken violin lessons for several months in Elizavetgrad, and he would strum occasionally. And at last, I too would play, with one finger, from my brother's violin music. I had no ear, and my love of music always remained helpless and unexpressed.

In the springtime the courtyard changed into a sea of mud. Ivan Vasilyevich would make a pair of wooden galoshes, or rather buskins, for himself, and I used to watch him with delight, striding along a foot above his usual height. In time the old saddler appears upon the scene. No one, it seems, knows his name. He is more than eighty years old and has served twenty-five years in the army of Nicholas I. Huge and broad-shouldered, with white beard and hair, he scarcely moves his heavy feet as he shuffles across to the barn, where his itinerant work-shop has been installed. "My legs are getting weak," he has been complaining for the past ten years. On the contrary, his hands, which smell of leather, are stronger than pincers. His nails resemble the ivory keys of the spinet, and are very sharp at the ends.

"Would you like me to show you Moscow?" asks the saddler. Of course I should! The old man puts his thumbs under my ears and raises me up. His dreadful nails press into me, and I am offended and hurt. I kick my heels and try to get down. "If you don't want to see Moscow, you needn't!" In spite of being offended, I do not run away. "Hello!" says the old man, climbing the barn stairs. "Look what's here in the loft!" I suspect a trick, and hesitate to go in. It turns out that Constantine, the youngest miller, is in the loft with Katy, the cook. Both are handsome, jolly, and hardworking. "When are you and Katy going to get married?" asks their mistress. "Why, we are getting on very well as we are," answers Constantine. "It costs ten roubles to get married, and I should rather buy Katy a pair of boots."

After the hot, tense summer of the steppe is over, and its toilsome climax of reaping and harvesting has passed, comes the early autumn to take stock of a year's penal labor. The threshing is now in full swing. The centre of activity has moved to the threshing-floor beyond the sheds, a quarter of a mile from the house. A cloud of dust floats over the threshing-floor. The drum of the thresher is whining. Philip the miller, wearing glasses, is standing beside it. His black beard is covered with gray dust. The men are carrying in sheaves from the wagon. He takes them without looking at them, unties them, shakes them apart, and throws them into the thresher. At each armful the thresher growls like a dog with a bone. The straw-shaker throws out the straw, playing with it as it goes. The chaff pours out of a pipe at the side and is carried to the straw stack on a drag, with me standing on its wooden tail-board and holding on by the rope reins. "Mind you don't fall!" cries my father. And down I go for the tenth time. I fall now into the straw, now into the chaff. The gray dust cloud thickens over the threshing-floor, the engine groans, the hulls get into one's shirt and nose and make one sneeze. "Hey, Philip! not so fast!" warns my father from below, as the thresher growls too fiercely. I lift the drag. It slips out of my hands and falls with its whole weight on my finger. The pain is so intense that my head swims. I slip to one side so that the men shall not see me crying, and then run home. My mother pours cold water on my hand and bandages my finger, but the pain does not diminish. The wound festers during several days of torture.

Sacks of wheat now fill the barns and the sheds, and are piled in heaps under tarpaulins in the courtyard. The master himself often stands at the sieve and shows the men how to turn the hoop, so as to blow away the chaff, and how, with one sharp push, to empty the clean grain into a pile without leaving any behind. In the sheds and barns, where there is shelter from the wind, the winnower and the tare-separators are working. The grain is cleaned there and made ready for the market.

And now merchants come with copper vessels and scales in neatly painted boxes. They test the grain and name a price, pressing earnest-money on my father. We treat them with respect and give them tea and cakes, but we do not sell them the grain. They are but small fry; the master has outgrown these channels of trade. He has his own commission merchant in Nikolayev. "Let it be awhile, grain doesn't ask to be fed!" he says.

A week later a letter comes from Nikolayev, or sometimes a telegram, offering five kopecks a pood more. "So we have found a thousand roubles!" says the master. "And they don't grow on every bush!" But sometimes the reverse happens; sometimes the price falls. The secret power of the world market makes itself felt even in Yanovka. Then my father says gloomily, returning from Nikolayev: "It seems that—what is the name?—the Argentine, sent out too much wheat this year."

Winter was a peaceful time in the country. Only the machine-shop and the mill were still really active. For fuel we burned straw which the servants brought in huge armfuls, scattering it along the way and sweeping it up after themselves. It was jolly to stuff this straw into the stoves and watch it blaze up. Once Uncle Gregory found my younger sister and me alone in the dining-room, which was filled with blue charcoal fumes. I was turning round and round in the middle of the room, not knowing where I was, and at my uncle's cry I fell in a dead faint. We often found ourselves alone in the house on winter days, especially during my father's absences, when all the work of the place fell on my mother. In the dusk my little sister and I used to sit side by side on the sofa, pressed close together, wide-eyed and afraid to move.

A giant would come out of the cold outside into the dark dining-room, shuffling his huge boots, and wrapped in an enormous greatcoat with a huge collar, and wearing a huge hat. His hands were encased in huge mittens. Large icicles hung from his beard and mustache, and his great voice would boom out in the darkness: "Good evening!" Squeezed together in a corner of the sofa, we would be afraid to answer him. Then the monster would light a match and see us in our corner. The giant would turn out to be one of our neighbors. Sometimes the loneliness in the dining-room became absolutely unbearable, and then I ran out into the outer hall in spite of the cold, opened the front door, stepped out onto the big stone that lay on the threshold, and screamed into the darkness: "Mashka! Mashka! Come into the dining-room!" over and over again. Mashka was busy with her own affairs in the kitchen, in the servants' room, or somewhere else. My mother would come in at last, perhaps from the mill, light a lamp, and the samovar would be brought in.

We usually sat in the dining-room in the evening until we fell asleep. People came and went in the dining-room, taking or returning keys, making arrangements of various kinds, and planning the work for the following day. My younger sister Olya, my older sister Liza, the chambermaid and myself then lived a life of our own, which was dependent on the life of the grown-ups, and subdued by theirs. Sometimes a chance word of one of the elders would waken some special reminiscence in us.

Then I would wink at my little sister, she would give a low giggle, and the grown-ups would look absent-mindedly at her. I would wink again, and she would try to stifle her laughter under the oilcloth and would hit her head against the table. This would infect me and sometimes my older sister too, who, with thirteen-year-old dignity, vacillated between the grown-ups and the children. If our laughter became too uncontrollable, I was obliged to slip under the table and crawl among the feet of the grown-ups, and, stepping on the cat's tail, rush out into the next room, which was the nursery. Once back in the dining-room, it all would begin over again. My fingers would grow so weak from laughing that I could not hold a glass. My head, my lips, my hands, my feet, every inch of me would be shaking with laughter. "Whatever is the matter with you?" my mother would ask. The two circles of life, the upper and the lower, would touch for a moment. The grown-ups would look at the children with a question in their eyes that was sometimes friendly but more often full of irritation. Then our laughter, taken unawares, would break out tempestuously into the open. Olya's head would go under the table again, I would throw myself on the sofa, Liza would bite her upper lip, and the chambermaid would slip out of the door.

"Go to bed!" the grown-ups would cry.

But we would not go. We would hide in corners, afraid to look at one another. My little sister would be carried away, but I usually went to sleep on the sofa. Some one would pick me up in his arms and take me out. Then I would perhaps give a loud yell, imagining, half-asleep, that I was being attacked by dogs, that snakes were hissing below me, or that robbers were carrying me away into the woods. The child's nightmare would break into the life of the grown-ups. I would be quieted on the way to bed; they would pat and kiss me. So I would go from laughter into sleep, from nightmares into wakefulness, and back into sleep again in a feather bed in the warm bedroom.

Winter was the family time of year. There came days when my mother and father hardly left the house. My older brother and sister came home for Christmas from their schools. On Sundays, Ivan Vasilyevich, all washed and shaved, and armed with a comb and scissors, would cut first my father's hair, then Sasha's, and then mine. Sasha asks:

"Can you cut hair *à la Capoul*, Ivan Vasilyevich?" Every one looks at Sasha, and he explains that in Elizavetgrad the barber once cut his hair beautifully *à la Capoul*, but that next day the supervisor gave him a severe reprimand.

After the hair-cutting is over, we sit down to dinner, my father and Ivan Vasilyevich in armchairs at each end of the table, the children on the sofa, and my mother opposite them. Ivan Vasilyevich took his meals with us until he was married. In winter we ate slowly and sat talking afterward. Ivan Vasilyevich would smoke and blow ingenious rings. Sometimes Sasha or Liza was made to read aloud. My father would doze in the recess of the stove. Once in a while in the evening we played old-maid, from which a great deal of noise and laughter resulted, and sometimes a little quarrelling. We thought it particularly amusing to cheat my father, who played carelessly, and laughed when he lost. My mother, on the other hand, played better, and would grow excited and watch my oldest brother sharply to see that he was not cheating her.

It was twenty-three kilometres from Yanovka to the nearest post-office, and more than thirty-five to the railroad. From there it was a long way again to the Government offices, to the stores and to a civic centre, and still farther to the world with its great events. Life at Yanovka was regulated entirely by the rhythm of the toil on the farm. Nothing else mattered, nothing but the price of grain in the world market. We never saw any magazines or newspapers in the country in those days. That followed later, when I had become a high-school boy. We got letters only on special occasions. Sometimes a neighbor would find a letter for us at Bobrinetz and carry it in his pocket for a week or two. A letter was an event; a telegram was a catastrophe. Some one explained to me that telegrams came on wires, but with my own eyes I saw a man on horseback bring a telegram from Bobrinetz for which my father had to pay two roubles and fifty kopecks. A telegram was a piece of paper, like a letter. There were words written on it in pencil. Did the wind blow it along a wire? I was told that it came by electricity. That was still worse. Uncle Abram once carefully explained to me: "The current comes over the wire and makes marks on a ribbon. Repeat what I have said." I repeated: "Current over the wire and marks on a ribbon."

"Do you understand?"

"Yes, I understand, but how do they make a letter out of it?" I asked, thinking of the telegraph blank which had come from Bobrinetz.

"The letter comes separately," my uncle answered. I puzzled for a moment and then asked: "And why do they need the current if the letter comes by a man on horseback?" But here my uncle lost patience. "Oh, let that letter alone!" he cried. "I try to explain to you about telegrams and you begin on letters!" So the question remained unanswered.

Paulina Petrovna, a lady from Bobrinetz, came to stay with us. She had long earrings and a curl on her forehead. Later my mother took her back to Bobrinetz and I went with them. When we had passed the mound that marks the eleventh verst, a row of telegraph poles appeared, and the wires were humming.

"How do telegrams come?" I asked my mother.

"Ask Paulina Petrovna," my mother answered, at a loss. "She will explain it to you."

Paulina Petrovna explained:

"The marks on the ribbon stand for letters. The operator copies them on paper, and the paper is sent by a man on horseback." I could understand that.

"But how can the current go without any one seeing it?" I asked, looking at the wire.

"The current goes inside," answered Paulina Petrovna. "All those wires are made like little tubes and the current runs along inside."

I could understand that too, and was satisfied for a long time afterward. The electro-magnetic fluid which my teacher of physics told me about four years later seemed a much less reasonable explanation to me.

My father and mother lived out their hard-working lives with some friction, but very happily on the whole. My mother came from a family of townspeople who looked down upon farmers, with their rough hands. But my father had been handsome and graceful in his youth, with a manly, energetic face. He succeeded in getting together the means that later enabled him to buy Yanovka. The young woman who had been taken from the city and flung out onto the lonely steppes found it difficult at first to adjust herself to the stern conditions of life on a farm. But she succeeded at last in adapting herself perfectly, and once in the traces, she did not relinquish her toil for forty-five years. Of the eight children born of this marriage, four survived. I was the fifth in order of birth. Four died in infancy, of diphtheria and of scarlet fever, deaths almost as unnoticed as was the life of those who survived. The land, the cattle, the poultry, the mill, took all my parents' time; there was none left for us. The seasons succeeded one another, and waves of farm work swept over domestic affection. There was no display of tenderness in our family, especially during my early years, but there was a strong comradeship of labor between my father and mother.

"Give your mother a chair!" my father would cry as soon as my mother crossed the threshold, white with dust from the mill.

"Mashka! Light the samovar quick," my mother would command even before she had reached the house. "Your master will soon be in from the fields." Both knew what it was to have reached the limit of physical exhaustion.

My father was undoubtedly superior to my mother, both in intellect and character. He was deeper, more reserved, and more tactful. He had an unusually good eye both for things and people. My father and mother bought very little, especially during our early years; they both knew how to save every penny. My father never made a mistake in what he bought: cloth, hats, shoes, horses or machinery, he always got his money's worth. "I don't like money," he once said to me later, as if apologizing for being so mean, "but I like it less when there is none of it. It is bad to need money and not have any." He spoke a broken mixture of the Russian and Ukrainian tongues, with a preponderance of the Ukrainian. He judged people by their manners, their faces and their habits, and he always judged them correctly.

"I don't like that student of yours," he would sometimes say of one of our guests. "Confess it, don't you yourself think he is an idiot?" Our feelings would be hurt for our guest's sake, but we knew in our hearts that our father was right. After visiting once in a family, he summed up the domestic situation there very correctly.

After bearing many children and after much hard work, my mother once fell ill, and went to see a doctor in Kharkoff. Such a journey was a great event, and many preparations were made for it. My mother went well supplied with money, jars of butter, bags of sweet biscuits, fried chicken and so forth. She had great expenses ahead of her. The doctor's fee was three roubles a visit. My mother and father always spoke of this to each other and to their guests with uplifted hands and an expression on their faces that signified their respect for the benefits of science, their regret that they cost so dear, and their pride that they were able to pay such an unheard-of price for them. We awaited my mother's return with great excitement. She came back in a new dress that looked incredibly grand in our dining-room at Yanovka.

When we children were young, my father was quieter and gentler with us than my mother. My mother would often lose her temper with us, sometimes without reason, and would vent on us her fatigue or her chagrin over some domestic failure. We always found it more remunerative to ask our father for favors than our mother. But as time went on, my father grew sterner. The cause of this lay in the hardships of his life, in the cares which grew as his business increased, and more especially in the conditions growing out of the agrarian crisis of the '80's, as well as in the disappointment which his children gave him.

My mother loved to read during the long winters, when Yanovka was swept by the snow drifting from all the corners of the steppe and rising over the windows. She would sit on a small three-cornered seat in the dining-room with her feet on a chair before her, or, when the early winter twilight fell, she would move into my father's armchair near the small, frosty window, and read in a loud whisper from some worn novel out of the library at Bobrinetz, following the words with her toil-worn finger. She often grew confused, and faltered over some especially long sentence. Sometimes an explanation from any one of the children would throw an entirely new light for her on the story she had been reading. But she continued to read perseveringly and untiringly, and on quiet winter days we could hear her monotonous whisper as far as the front hall.

My father learned to spell out words even when he was quite an old man, in order to be able to read at least the titles of my books. I followed him with excitement in Berlin in 1910, when he perseveringly tried to understand my book on German Social Democracy.

The October Revolution found my father a very prosperous man. My mother had died in 1910, but my father lived to see the rule of the Soviets. At the height of the civil war, which raged with especial fury in the South and was accompanied by constant changes of government, the old man of seventy was obliged to walk hundreds of miles to find shelter in Odessa. The Reds were a menace to him because he was rich; the Whites persecuted him because he was my father. After the South had been freed of White soldiers by the Soviet troops, he was enabled to come to Moscow. He had lost all his savings in the Revolution. For more than a year he ran a small state mill near Moscow. The Commissar of Food at that time, Tzyurupa, used to enjoy chatting with him on agricultural subjects. My father died of typhus in the spring of 1922, at the very moment when I was reading my report at the Fourth Congress of the Communist International.

A very important, in fact, the most important, place at Yanovka was the machine-shop, where Ivan Vasilyevich Gryeben worked. He came to work there when he was twenty, the year that I was born. He addressed all the children, even the older ones, as "thou," while we spoke to him respectfully as "you." When he had to report for military service my father went with him. They gave some one a bribe, and Gryeben stayed at Yanovka. This Ivan Vasilyevich was handsome and gifted. He wore a dark reddish mustache and a beard cut in the French fashion. His technical knowledge was comprehensive. He could rebuild an engine, repair a boiler, turn a metal or a wooden ball, cast a brass bearing, make a spring carriage, mend a clock, tune a piano, upholster furniture, or make a bicycle minus the tires. It was on a bicycle of his manufacture that I learned to ride in the year when I was between the primary and first grades. The neighboring German settlers would bring in their seed-drills and binders to be repaired by him, and would invite him to go with them to buy a threshing-machine or a steam-engine. People came to my father for advice about farming, and to Ivan Vasilyevich for advice about machinery. There were assistants as well as apprentices employed in the machine-shop. In many ways I was the pupil of these apprentices.

I was sometimes allowed to cut the threads of nuts and screws in the machine-shop. I liked this work because I could see the direct result in my hands. I sometimes tried to grind the material for paint on a round, smooth stone, but I soon tired, and would ask more and more frequently whether the work was nearly finished. Stirring the thick mixture with his finger, Ivan Vasilyevich would shake his head, and I would hand over the stone to one of the apprentices.

Ivan Vasilyevich would sometimes sit down on a chest in the corner behind the work-bench, a tool in hand. He would smoke and gaze into the distance, perhaps pondering something or remembering something or simply resting without thinking at all. At such times I used to sit down beside him and gently curl his thick, auburn mustache around my finger, or examine his hands, those unmistakable hands of the artisan. Their skin was all covered with little black spots that he had got from cutting millstones. His fingers were as tenacious as roots, but not hard. They were broad at the tips but very supple, and his thumb turned far backward, forming an arch. Each finger was self-conscious, and lived and acted by itself, but together they formed a very effective labor-union. I was still quite young, but already I could feel that that hand did not hold a hammer or a pair of pliers as other hands did. A deep scar encircled his left thumb. Ivan Vasilyevich had very nearly cut it off with a hatchet the day I was born. It was hanging almost by the skin alone. My father had happened to see the young mechanic lay his hand on a board, about to chop his thumb off altogether. "Stop a moment!" he had cried. "Your finger will grow on again!"

"It will grow on again, you think?" the mechanic had asked, and laid the hatchet aside. And the thumb had grown on, and again worked well, except that it did not turn back as far as the other.

Ivan Vasilyevich once made a shotgun out of an old Berdan rifle and tried his skill at marksmanship. Every one in turn tried at a distance of several paces to put out a candle by striking the primer. Not every one succeeded. My father chanced to pass by. When he raised the gun to his shoulder, his hands trembled and he held it without assurance. But he put the candle out at the first trial. He had a good eye for everything, and Ivan Vasilyevich knew this. There were never any altercations between them, though my father would scold the other workmen and find fault with their work.

I never lacked occupation in the machine-shop. I would tug the handle of the blower which Ivan Vasilyevich had made according to a plan of his own. The ventilator was out of sight in the loft, and this excited surprise in every one who saw it. I would turn the lathe till I was exhausted, especially when croquet-balls of acacia wood were being made. The conversations that took place in the machine-shop seemed each more interesting than the last. Propriety did not always rule there—or rather I might say that it never ruled there. My horizon was widened there hourly. Foma told stories about the estate where he used to work, and about the adventures of the ladies and gentlemen there. I must say that he was not very complimentary to them. Philip, the miller, would follow with stories of army life. Ivan Vasilyevich would ask questions, restrain the others, or supplement what they said.

The fireman Yashka was a surly, red-haired man of thirty who never kept any position for long. Something would come over him, and he would disappear either in the spring or in the autumn, and return six months later. He did not drink often, but periodically. He passionately loved hunting, but nevertheless he sold his gun for drink. Foma told how Yashka had come into a store in Bobrinetz barefooted, his feet plastered with black mud, and had asked for a box of caps. He purposely spilled the caps on the floor, and stooped to pick them up. In doing so, he stepped on some of them with his muddy feet, and went out taking them with him.

"Is Foma lying?" asked Ivan Vasilyevich.

"Why do you think he is lying?" asked Yashka. "I hadn't a penny to pay for them."

This seemed to me a good way of getting something you wanted, and one worthy of imitation.

"Our Ignat has come," Mashka, the housemaid, came in to tell us. "But Dunka isn't here, she has gone home for the holiday."

We called the fireman Ignat "our" Ignat, to distinguish him from humpbacked Ignat, who had been an Elder before Taras came. "Our" Ignat had gone to be drafted for military service—Ivan Vasilyevich himself had measured his chest and had said, "They wouldn't take him for anything!" The examination board put Ignat into the hospital for a month, on trial. There he made the acquaintance of some workmen from the city, and resolved to try his luck in a factory. When he came back he was wearing city boots and a sheepskin coat with a front embroidered in colors. Ignat spent the whole day after his return in the machine-shop, telling the men about the city and about the work, conditions, machinery and wages he had found there.

"Of course, it's a factory," began Foma meditatively.

"A factory isn't a machine-shop!" observed Philip. And they all looked thoughtful, as if seeing beyond the machine-shop.

"Is there much machinery in the city?" asked Victor eagerly.

"A whole forest of it!"

I listened with all my ears, and saw in my mind's eye a factory with machines in it as thick as trees in a forest; machines to the right, to the left, before, behind; machines everywhere. And in the midst of it all I pictured Ignat standing with a tight leather belt round his waist. Ignat had also acquired a watch, which was passed from hand to hand. In the evening, Ignat walked up and down the courtyard with my father, followed by the steward. I was there too, running now beside my father and now beside Ignat.

"Well, and how do you live?" asked my father, "Do you buy your bread and milk? Do you rent a room?"

"To be sure, you have to pay for absolutely everything," Ignat assented, "but the wages aren't the same as they are here."

"I know they aren't the same, but they all go for food."

"No," answered Ignat stoutly. "I have been able to save enough in six months to buy some clothes and a watch. Here it is in my pocket." And he pulled out his watch again. The argument was unanswerable, and my father said nothing. Then he asked again:

"Have you been drinking, Ignat? With so many teachers around you it should not be hard to learn!"

"Why, I never even think of vodka."

"And are you going to take Dunka back with you, Ignat?" my mother asked him.

Ignat smiled a little guiltily and did not answer.

"Oh, I see, I see," said my mother. "So you have already found some city slut! Confess to it, you scoundrel!"

So Ignat went away again from Yanovka.

We children were forbidden to go into the servants' room, but who could prevent our doing so? There was always much that was new there. Our cook for a long time was a woman with high cheek-bones and a sunken nose. Her husband, who was an old man and was paralyzed down one side of his face, was our shepherd. We called them Muscovites because they came from one of the governments of the interior. This couple

23

had a pretty little daughter eight years old, with blue eyes and blond hair. She was used to seeing her father and mother forever quarrelling.

On Sundays the girls used to hunt for lice in the boys' hair or in their own. On a pile of straw in the servants' room the two Tatyanas would be lying side by side, Big Tatyana and Little Tatyana. Afanasy, the stable boy, son of Pud the steward and brother to Paraska, the cook, would sit down between them, throwing his leg over Little Tatyana and leaning against Big Tatyana.

"What a Mohammedan you are!" the young steward would cry enviously. "Isn't it time to water the horses?"

This red-haired Afanasy and the black-haired Mutuzok were my persecutors. If I chanced to come in while the pudding or the porridge was being handed around, they would cry laughingly: "Come on, Lyova, and have dinner with us!" or, "Why don't you ask your mother for a bit of chicken for us, Lyova?" I would feel embarrassed and go out without answering. At Easter my mother was wont to bake cakes for the workmen and color eggs for them. Aunt Raisa was an artist at painting eggs. She once brought some gaily painted eggs with her from Gromokley and gave me two. We used to roll our eggs down the slides behind the cellar to see which was the strongest. Once I was left to the end; only Afanasy and I remained.

"Aren't these pretty?" I asked, showing him my painted eggs.

"Yes, they are pretty enough," answered Afanasy, with an air of indifference. "Let me see which is the strongest."

I did not dare to refuse the challenge. Afanasy struck my egg and it cracked on top.

"So that one is mine!" said Afanasy. "Now let's try the other." I obediently offered him my second painted egg.

Afanasy struck again.

"That one is mine too!"

Afanasy picked up both eggs in a businesslike way and went off without looking back. I watched him go in astonishment, and felt very much like crying, but there was nothing to be done about it.

There were very few permanent laborers who worked all the year round on the estate. Most of them—and there were hundreds of these on the estate in years of large crops—were temporary only, and comprised men from Kiev, Chernigov, and Poltava, who were hired until the first of October. In the years when the harvest was good, the Province of Kherson alone would require two or three hundred thousand of these laborers. The reapers received forty to fifty roubles for the four summer months, and their board. The women received from twenty to thirty roubles. The open field was their home in fine weather, in bad weather they took shelter under the haystacks. For dinner they had vegetable soup and porridge, for supper millet soup. They never had any meat. Vegetable fat was all they ever got, and that in small quantities. This diet was sometimes a ground for complaint. The laborers would leave the fields and collect in the courtyard. They would lie face downward in the shade of the barns, brandishing their bare, cracked, straw-pricked feet in the air, and wait to see what would happen. Then my father would give them some clabber, or watermelons, or half a sack of dried fish, and they would go back to work again, often singing. These were the conditions on all the farms. We had wiry old reapers who had been coming to work for us ten years on end, knowing that work was always assured them. These received a few roubles more than the others and a glass of vodka from time to time, as they set the standard of efficiency for the others. Some of them appeared at the head of a long family procession. They walked from their own provinces on foot, taking a whole month to make the journey, living on crusts of bread, and spending the nights in the market-places. One summer all the laborers fell ill in an epidemic of night-blindness. They moved about in the twilight with their hands stretched out before them. My mother's nephew, who was visiting us, wrote an article to the newspapers about it. It was spoken of in the Zemstvo, and an inspector was sent to Yanovka. My father and mother were vexed with the newspaper correspondent, who was much liked, and he himself was sorry that he had begun it. Nothing unpleasant came of it all, however. The inspector decided that the sickness was due to a lack of fat in the diet, and that it was common all over the province, as the laborers were fed in the same manner everywhere, and sometimes even worse.

In the machine-shop, the kitchen, and the backyard, a life stretched before me which was different from and more spacious than the one I led in my own family. The film of life has no end, and I was only at the beginning. No one took any notice of my presence when I was little. Tongues wagged freely, especially when Ivan Vasilyevich and the steward were absent, for they half belonged to the ruling class. By the light of the blacksmith's forge or the kitchen fire, I often saw my parents, my relatives and our neighbors in quite a new light. Many of the conversations I overheard when I was young will remain in my memory as long as I live. Many of them, perhaps, laid the foundation of my attitude toward society to-day.

CHAPTER II

OUR NEIGHBORS AND MY FIRST SCHOOL

A VERST or less from Yanovka lay the property of the Dembovskys. My father leased land from them and was connected with them by many business ties. Theodosia Antonovna, the owner, was an old Polish woman who had once been a governess. After the death of her first rich husband, she married her manager, Kasimir Antonovich, who was twenty years younger than herself. Theodosia Antonovna had not lived with her second husband for years, though he still managed the property. Kasimir Antonovich was a tall, bearded, noisy and jolly Pole. He often had tea with us at the big oval table, and would uproariously tell the same silly story over and over again, repeating individual words and emphasizing them by snapping his fingers.

Kasimir Antonovich kept some hives of bees at a distance from the stable and cowsheds, since bees cannot bear the smell of horses. The bees made honey from the fruit-trees, the white acacias, the winter rape, and the buckwheat—in a word, they were in the midst of abundance. From time to time Kasimir Antonovich would bring us two plates covered with a napkin, between which lay a piece of honeycomb full of clear, golden honey.

One day Ivan Vasilyevich and I went together to get some pigeons for breeding purposes from Kasimir Antonovich. In a corner room of the great empty house, Kasimir Antonovich gave us tea, butter, honey, and curds on large plates that smelled damp. I sat drinking tea out of my saucer and listening to the lagging conversation. "Shan't we be late?" I whispered to Ivan Vasilyevich. "No, wait a little longer. We must give them time to settle down in their loft. You can see them up there still." I grew weary. At last we climbed up into the loft over the barn, carrying a lantern. "Look out now!" cried Kasimir Antonovich to me. The loft was long and dark, with rafters in all directions. It had a strong smell of mice, bees, cobwebs and birds. Some one put out the lantern. "There

27

they are! Grab them!" Kasimir Antonovich whispered. An infernal uproar broke loose; the loft was filled with a whirl-wind of wings. It seemed to me for a moment that the end of the world had come, and that we were all lost. Gradually I came to, and heard an anxious voice saying: "Here's another! This way, this way—that's right, put him in the sack." Ivan Vasilyevich had brought a sack along, and all the way back we had behind us a continuation of the scene in the loft. We made a pigeon-loft over the machine-shop. I climbed up there ten times a day after that, taking water, wheat, millet and crumbs to the pigeons. A week later I found two eggs in a nest. But before we were able fully to appreciate this important event, the pigeons began to return to their old home, one pair at a time. Only three pairs who had had their wings cut were left behind, and these flew away too when their wings had grown out, leaving the beautiful loft we had made for them, with its nests and its system of halls. Thus ended our venture in raising pigeons.

My father leased some land near Elizavetgrad from Mrs. T., who was a widow of forty with a strong character. In constant attendance on her was a priest, also widowed, who was a lover of cards and of music and of many other things beside. Mrs. T., accompanied by the priest, once came to Yanovka to see about the terms of our contract with her. We assigned the sitting-room and the room adjoining it to them, and gave them fried chicken, cherry wine and cherry dumplings for dinner. After the meal was over, I stayed in the parlor and saw the priest sit down beside her and laughingly whisper something into her ear. Turning back the front of his coat, he took a silver cigarette-case with a monogram out of the pocket of his striped trousers and lit a cigarette, lightly blowing rings of smoke. He then told us, while his mistress was out of the room, that she read only the dialogue in novels. Every one smiled politely, but refrained from criticism, for we knew that he would not only repeat it to her, but add to it something of his own invention.

My father began to lease land from Mrs. T. in partnership with Kasimir Antonovich. The latter's wife died at about this time, and a sudden change occurred in him. The gray hairs disappeared from his beard; he wore a starched collar, and a tie with a tie-pin, and carried a lady's photograph in his pocket. Although, like every one else, Kasimir Antonovich laughed at my Uncle Gregory, it was to him that he turned in all affairs of the heart. He took the photograph out of its envelope and showed it to him.

"Look!" he cried to Uncle Gregory, almost fainting with ecstasy. "I said to this beautiful being: 'Lady, your lips are made for kisses!'" Kasimir Antonovich married the beautiful being, but he died suddenly after a year and a half of married life. A bull caught him on his horns in the courtyard of the T. estate and gored him to death.

The brothers F. owned a property of thousands of acres about eight versts from ours. Their house resembled a palace and was richly furnished, with many guest-rooms, a billiard-room and much beside. The two F. brothers, Lev and Ivan, had inherited all this from their father Timothy, and were gradually going through their inheritance. The administration of the property was in the hands of a steward, and the books showed a deficit, in spite of double-entry bookkeeping.

"Davyd Leontiyevich is richer than I am, if he does live in a mud house!" the elder brother would say of my father, and when we repeated this to my father, he was obviously pleased. The younger brother, Ivan, once rode through Yanovka with two of his huntsmen, their guns on their backs, and a pack of white wolfhounds at their heels. This had never been seen before at Yanovka.

"They will soon go through their money at that rate!" said my father disapprovingly.

The seal of doom was on these families of the Province of Kherson. They were all progressing with extraordinary rapidity, and all in the same direction: toward downfall. And this was true in spite of the many differences between them, for some belonged to the hereditary nobility, some were Government officials endowed with land for their services, some were Poles, some were Germans, and some were Jews who had been able to buy land before 1881. The founders of many of these steppe dynasties were men prominent in their way, successful, and robbers by nature.

I had never known any of them, however, as they had all died during the early '80's. Many of them had begun life with a broken penny but with the knack of cleverness, even if it was sometimes that of a criminal, and they had acquired tremendous possessions. The second generation of these people grew up as a new-made aristocracy, with a knowledge of French, with billiard-rooms in their houses, with all sorts of bad ways to their credit. The agricultural crisis of the '80's, brought on by trans-Atlantic competition, hit them unmercifully. They fell like dead leaves. The third generation produced a lot of half-rotten scoundrels, worthless fellows, unbalanced, premature invalids.

The highest peak of aristocratic ruin was reached in the Ghertopanov family. A large village and a whole county were called by their name. The whole countryside had once belonged to them. The old heir to it all had now only one thousand acres left, and these were mortgaged over and over again. My father leased this land, and the rents went into the bank. Ghertopanov lived by writing petitions, complaints and letters for the peasants. When he came to see us he used to hide tobacco and lumps of sugar up his sleeve, and his wife did the same. With drivelling lips she would tell us stories of her youth, with its serfs, its grand pianos, its silks and its perfumery. Their two sons grew up almost illiterate. The younger, Victor, was an apprentice in our machine-shop.

A family of Jewish landowners lived about six versts from Yanovka. Their name was M——sky. They were a queer, mad lot. Their father, Moissey Kharitonovich, was sixty years old, and was distinguished by having received an education of the aristocratic variety. He spoke French fluently, played the piano, and knew something about literature. His left hand was weak, but his right hand was fit, he said, to play in a concert. His neglected finger-nails, striking the keys of our old spinet, made a noise like castanets. Beginning with a Polonaise by Oginsky, he would pass imperceptibly into a Rhapsody by Liszt and suddenly slip into the "Maiden's Prayer"; his conversation was equally erratic. He would often stop in the midst of his playing and get up and go to the mirror. Then, if no one was by, he would singe his beard on all sides with his burning cigarette, with the idea of keeping it tidy. He smoked incessantly, and sighed as he did so, as if he disliked it. He had not spoken to his heavy, old wife for fifteen years.

30

His son David was thirty-five years old. He invariably wore a white bandage over one side of his face, showing above it a red, twitching eye. David was an unsuccessful suicide. When he was in military service, he had insulted an officer on duty. His officer had struck him. David gave the officer a slap in the face, ran into the barracks, and tried to shoot himself with his rifle. The bullet went through his cheek, and for that reason he now wore that inevitable white bandage. The guilty soldier was threatened with a stern court martial, but the patriarch of the house of M——sky was still alive at that time— old Khariton, rich, powerful, illiterate, despotic. He roused the whole countryside and had his grandson declared irresponsible. Perhaps, after all, it was not far from the truth! From that time on, David lived with a pierced cheek and the passport of a lunatic.

The M——sky family were still on the downward path at the time I first knew them. During my earliest years, Moissey Kharitonovich used to come to see us in a phaeton drawn by fine carriage horses. When I was tiny, perhaps four or five years old, I visited the M——sky family with my oldest brother. They had a large, well-kept garden, with—actually!— peacocks walking about in it. I saw these marvellous creatures there for the first time in my life, with crowns on their capricious heads, lovely little mirrors in their tails, and spurs on their legs. The peacocks vanished in after years, and much more went with them; the garden fence fell to pieces, the cattle broke down the fruit-trees and the flowers. Moissey Kharitonovich now came to Yanovka in a wagon drawn by farm horses. The sons made an effort to bring the property up, but as farmers, not as gentlemen. "We shall buy some old nags and drive them in the morning, as Bronstein does!"

"They won't succeed!" said my father. David was sent to the Fair at Elizavetgrad to buy the "old nags." He walked about the Fair, appraising the horses with the eye of a cavalryman, and chose a troika. He came home late in the evening. The house was full of guests in their light summer clothes. Abram went out onto the porch with a lamp in his hand to look at the horses. A crowd of ladies, students and young people followed him. David suddenly felt that he was in his element and extolled the good points of each horse, especially of the

one which he said resembled a young lady. Abram scratched
his beard and said: "The horses are all right." It ended in a
picnic. David took the slippers off a pretty young lady, filled
them with beer, and held them to his lips.

"You aren't going to drink it?" cried the girl, blushing either
with alarm or with delight.

"If I wasn't afraid to shoot myself—" answered our hero,
pouring the contents of the slipper down his throat.

"Don't always be boasting of that exploit of yours!" unexpectedly retorted his usually silent mother. She was a big,
flabby woman on whom fell all the burden of the household.

"Is that winter wheat?" Abram M——sky once inquired of
my father, to show how shrewd he was.

"Not spring wheat, certainly."

"Is it Nikopol wheat?"

"I tell you it is winter wheat."

"I know it is winter wheat, but what variety is it? Nikopol
or Girka?"

"Somehow or other I have never heard of Nikopol winter
wheat. Perhaps somebody has it, but I haven't got it. Mine
is Sandomir wheat," my father answered.

Nothing came of the sons' efforts. A year later my father
was leasing their land from them again.

The German settlers constituted a group apart. There were
some really rich men among them. They stood more firmly
on their feet than the others. Their domestic relations were
stricter, their sons were seldom sent to be educated in town,
their daughters habitually worked in the fields. Their houses
were built of brick with iron roofs painted green or red, their
horses were well bred, their harness was strong, their spring
carts were called "German wagons." Our nearest neighbor
among the Germans was Ivan Ivanovich Dorn, a fat, active
man with low shoes on his bare feet, with a tanned and bristling
face, and gray hair. He always drove about in a fine, bright-
painted wagon drawn by black stallions whose hoofs thundered
over the ground. And there were many of these Dorns.

Above them all towered the figure of Falz-Fein the Sheep
King, a "Kannitverstan" of the steppes.

In driving through the country, one would pass a huge flock
of sheep. "Whom do these belong to?" one would ask. "To

Falz-Fein." You met a hay-wagon on the road. Whom was that hay for? "For Falz-Fein." A pyramid of fur dashes by in a sleigh. It is Falz-Fein's manager. A string of camels suddenly startles you with its bellowing. Only Falz-Fein owns camels. Falz-Fein had imported stallions from America and bulls from Switzerland.

The founder of this family, who was called only Falz in those days, without the Fein, had been a shepherd on the estate of the Duke of Oldenburg. Oldenburg had been granted a large sum of money by the government for the breeding of Merino sheep. The duke made about a million of debts and did nothing. Falz bought the property and managed it like a shepherd and not like a duke. His flocks increased as well as his pastures and his business. His daughter married a sheep-breeder called Fein, and the two pastoral dynasties were thus united. The name of Falz-Fein rang like the sound of the feet of ten thousand sheep in motion, like the bleating of countless sheep voices, like the sound of the whistle of a shepherd of the steppes with his long crook on his back, like the barking of many sheep-dogs. The very steppe breathed this name both in summer heat and winter cold.

The first five years of my life are behind me. I am gaining experience. Life is full of invention, and is just as industrious at working out its combinations in an obscure little corner as it is on the world arena. Events crowd upon me, one after another.

A working girl is brought in bitten by a snake in the field. The girl is weeping piteously. They bandage her swollen leg tightly above the knee and bathe it in a barrel of sour milk. The girl is taken away to Bobrinetz, to the hospital. She returns and is at work again. On her bitten leg is a stocking, dirty and tattered, and the workingmen will call her nothing but "lady."

The boar-pig gnawed at the forehead, shoulders and arms of the man who was feeding him. It was a new, huge boar-pig that had been brought in to improve the entire herd of pigs. The fellow was frightened to death and sobbed like a boy. He too was taken to the hospital.

Two young workmen standing on wagon-loads of sheaves of

grain tossed pitchforks to each other. I fairly devoured this scene. One of them fell down moaning with a pitchfork in his side.

All this happened in the course of one summer. And no summer passed without its events.

One autumn night the entire wooden superstructure of the mill was swept into the pond. The piles had long since rotted, and the board walls were carried away like sails by the hurricane. The engine, the millstones, the coarse-grain grinder, the tare-separator stood out starkly in the ruins. From under the boards enormous mill-rats would dash out now and then.

Stealthily I would follow the water-carrier into the field to hunt marmots. With precision, not too rapidly and not too slowly, one would pour water into the burrow and await, with stick in hand, the appearance at the opening of the rat-like snout with its matted wet hair. An old marmot would resist a long time, stopping up the burrow with his rump, but a second bucket of water would make him surrender and jump out to meet his death. One had to cut off the paws of the dead animal and string them on a thread—the Zemstvo* would pay one kopeck for each marmot. They used to demand to be shown the tail, but clever fellows learned to make a dozen tails out of the skin of one animal; so the Zemstvo now required the paws. I would return all wet and dirty. At home such adventures were not encouraged. They preferred me to sit on the divan in the dining-room and draw the blind Œdipus and Antigone.

One day my mother and I were returning on a sleigh from Bobrinetz, the nearest town. Blinded by the snow, lulled by the ride, I was drowsy. The sleigh overturned on a curve and I fell face downward. The rug and the hay smothered me. I heard the alarmed cries of my mother but was unable to answer. The driver, a large, red-headed young fellow who was new, lifted the rug and found me. We resumed our seats and continued on our way. But I began to complain that chills were running up and down my spine. "Chills?" asked the red-bearded driver, turning his face to me and showing his firm white teeth. Looking at his mouth I answered: "Yes, you know, chills." The driver laughed. "It's nothing," he added,

* An elective rural organization in charge of the administration of country districts.—*Translator.*

34

"we'll be there soon!" and he urged on the light-bay horse. The following night that very driver vanished, together with the bay horse. There was a great to-do on the estate. A posse headed by my elder brother was quickly organized. He saddled Mutz, promising to mete out cruel punishment to the thief. "You better catch him first!" my father suggested gloomily. Two days passed before the posse returned. My brother blamed the fog for his not catching the horse-thief. A handsome jolly fellow with white teeth—such is a horse-thief!

I suffered from fever and tossed about. My arms, legs and head were in the way; they seemed inflated, pressing against the wall and the ceiling, and there was no escape from all these impediments because they sprang from within. I was all aflame; my throat pained. My mother looked into it, then my father did the same; they exchanged alarmed glances and decided to apply some salve to the throat. "I am afraid," Mother said, "that Lyova has diphtheria."

"If it had been diphtheria," replied Ivan Vasilyevich, "he would have been on the stretcher long ago."

Vaguely I surmised that lying on the stretcher meant being dead, as had been the case with my younger sister Rozochka. But I could not believe that they were speaking of me, and listened calmly to their talk. In the end it was decided to take me to Bobrinetz. My mother was not very orthodox, but on the Sabbath day she would not travel to town. Ivan Vasilyevich accompanied me. We put up at the house of Little Tatyana, our former servant, who had married in Bobrinetz. She had no children, and therefore there was no danger of contagion. Dr. Shatunovsky examined my throat, took my temperature, and as usual asserted that it was too early to know anything. Tatyana gave me a beer-bottle in the interior of which a complete little church had been constructed out of tiny sticks and boards. My legs and arms ceased to bother me. I recovered. When did this occur? Not long before the beginning of the new era in my life.

That came about in this way. Uncle Abram, an old egotist, who would neglect the children for weeks, called me over in a bright moment and asked: "Now tell me, without mincing words, what year is it? Ah, you don't know? It's 1885! Repeat that and remember it, for I'll ask you again." I could not comprehend the meaning of the question. "Yes, it's 1885 now," said my first cousin, the quiet Olga, "and then it will be 1886." This I could not believe. If one admitted that time had a name, then 1885 should exist forever, that is, very, very long, like that large stone at the threshold of the house, like the mill, or in fact like myself. Betya, the younger sister of Olga, did not know whom to believe. The three of us all felt disturbed at the thought of entering a new realm, as if some one had suddenly thrown open a door leading into a dark, empty room where voices echoed loudly. At last I had to yield. Everybody sided with Olga. And so 1885 became the first numbered year in my consciousness. It put an end to the formless, prehistoric, chaotic epoch of my earlier life: from now on I knew a chronology. I was six years old at the time. It was a year of crop failures, of crises, and of the first large labor disturbances in Russia. But it was the incomprehensible name of the year that had struck me. Apprehensively I endeavored to divine the hidden relation between time and numbers. There followed a series of years which moved slowly at first and then faster and faster. But 1885 stood out amongst them as an elder does, as the head of the clan. It marked an era.

The following incident stands out. I once climbed into the driver's seat of our baggage-wagon and, while waiting for my father, picked up the reins. The young horses raced off and made for the estate of the Dembovskys, flying past the house, the barn, the garden, and across the roadless field. There were cries behind and a ditch ahead. The horses tore on. Only on the very edge of the ditch, with a swerve which almost upset the wagon, did they stop as if rooted to the spot. After us came running the driver, followed by two or three laborers and my father. My mother was screaming, my elder sister was wringing her hands. My mother went on screaming even while I was dashing over to her. It should also be recorded that my father, deathly pale, treated me to a couple of slaps. I was not even offended, so extraordinary did it all seem.

It must have been in the same year that I accompanied my father on a trip to Elizavetgrad. We started at dawn, and went slowly. In Bobrinetz the horses were fed. We reached

Vshivaya* in the evening. We called it Shvivaya out of delicacy. There we stayed until daybreak, as robbers were reported on the outskirts. Not a single capital in the world, neither Paris nor New York, made in after years such an impression on me as Elizavetgrad with its sidewalks, green roofs, balconies, shops, policemen and red balloons. For several hours, with my eyes wide open, I gaped at the face of civilization.

A year later I began to study. One morning, after getting up and washing hastily—one always washed hastily in Yanovka—I entered the dining-room, looking forward to the new day and, above all, to the breakfast of tea with milk and buttered cake. I found my mother there in the company of a stranger, a lean, wanly smiling, obsequious man. My mother and the stranger looked at me in a way that made it clear that I had been the subject of their conversation.

"Shake hands, Lyova," said my mother. "Meet your teacher." I looked at the teacher with some fear, but not without interest. The teacher greeted me with that mildness with which every teacher greets his future pupil in the presence of parents. Mother completed the business arrangements right before me: for so many roubles and so many sacks of flour the teacher undertook to instruct me at his school in the colony, in Russian, arithmetic, and the Old Testament in the original Hebrew. The extent of the instruction, however, was left rather vague, as my mother was none too competent in such matters. Sipping my tea with milk, I seemed to taste the coming change in my destiny.

The following Sunday my father took me to the colony and placed me with Aunt Rachel. At the same time we brought her a load of produce, including wheat flour, barley flour, buckwheat, and millet.

The distance from Gromokley to Yanovka was four versts. Through the colony ran a ravine: on the one side was the Jewish settlement, on the other, the German. The two parts stood out in sharp contrast. In the German section the houses were neat, partly roofed with tile and partly with reeds, the horses large, the cows sleek. In the Jewish section the cabins were dilapidated, the roofs tattered, the cattle scrawny.

It is strange that my first school left very few impressions:

* In the Russian this means "lousy."—*Translator.*

a slate blackboard on which I first traced the letters of the Russian alphabet; the skinny index-finger of the teacher holding a pen; the reading of the Bible in unison; the punishment of some boy for stealing—all vague fragments, misty bits, not a single vivid picture. Perhaps the exception was the wife of the teacher, a tall, portly woman who from time to time took a part in our school life, always unexpectedly. Once during a session she complained to her husband that the new flour had a peculiar odor, and when he put his sharp nose to her handful of flour, she threw it in his face. That was her idea of a joke. The boys and girls laughed. Only the teacher looked downcast. I pitied him, standing in the midst of his class with a powdered face.

I lived with my good Aunt Rachel without being aware of her. On the same courtyard, in the main house, Uncle Abram ruled. He treated his nephews and nieces with complete indifference. Once in a while he would single me out, invite me in and treat me to a bone with marrow, adding: "I wouldn't take ten roubles for this bone."

My uncle's house was almost at the entrance to the colony. At the opposite end lived a tall, dark, thin Jew who had the name of being a horse-thief and of carrying on unsavory deals. He had a daughter—she too had a dubious reputation. Not far from the horse-thief lived the cap-maker, stitching away on his machine—a young Jew with a fiery red beard. The wife of the cap-maker would come to the official inspector of the colony, who always stayed at the house of Uncle Abram, to complain against the daughter of the horse-thief for stealing her husband. Apparently the inspector offered no aid. Returning from school one day, I saw a mob dragging a young woman, the daughter of the horse-thief, through the street. The mob was shouting, screaming, and spitting at her. This biblical scene was engraved on my memory forever. Several years later Uncle Abram married this very woman. By that time her father, by action of the colonies, had been exiled to Siberia as an undesirable member of the community.

My former nurse Masha was a servant in the home of Uncle Abram. I frequently ran to her in the kitchen; she symbolized my bond with Yanovka. Masha had visitors, sometimes rather impatient ones, and then I would be gently ushered out. One bright morning I learned, together with the rest of the children in the colony, that Masha had given birth to a baby. With great relish we whispered about it secretly. A few days later my mother arrived from Yanovka and went to the kitchen to see Masha and the child. I sneaked in behind my mother. Masha was wearing a kerchief which came down to her eyes. On a wide bench was the tiny creature, lying on its side. My mother looked at Masha, then at the child, and then shook her head reproachfully, saying nothing. Masha continued silent, with eyes downcast; then she looked at the infant and said: "Look how he puts his little hand under his cheek like a grown-up."

"Don't you pity him?" my mother asked.

"No," replied Masha deceitfully, "he is so sweet."

"It's a lie, you are sorry," retorted my mother in a conciliatory tone. The tiny infant died a week later as mysteriously as it had come into the world.

I often left school and returned to my village, remaining there almost a week at a time. I had no intimate friends among my schoolmates, as I did not speak Yiddish. The school season lasted only a few months. All of which may explain the paucity of my recollections of this period. And yet Shufer—that was the name of the Gromokley teacher—had taught me to read and write, both of which stood me in good stead in my later life, and for that reason I remember my first teacher with gratitude.

I began to make my way through lines of print. I copied verse. I even wrote verse myself. Later on I started a magazine, together with my cousin, Senya Z. And yet the new path was a thorny one. Scarcely had I mastered the art of writing when it seduced me. Once, while alone in the dining-room, I began to put down in printed script such special words as I had heard in the shop and in the kitchen and which I had never heard from my family. I realized that I was doing something which I should not be doing, but the words lured me just because they were forbidden. I had decided to hide the little paper in an empty match-box and then to bury it behind the barn. I was far from completing the list when my elder sister entered the room, and became interested. I seized the paper. My mother came in after my sister. They demanded that I show them the writing. Burning with shame, I threw the paper behind the divan. My sister tried to reach for it, but I cried out hysterically: "I'll get it myself." I crawled under the divan and there tore the paper into bits. There were no bounds to my despair, nor to my tears.

It must have been during Christmas week of 1886, because I already knew how to write at the time, that a troop of mummers tumbled into the dining-room one evening while we were at tea. It was so sudden that I fell on the divan from fright. I was quieted, and listened avidly to "Czar Maximilian." For the first time a fantastic world was revealed to me, a world transformed into a theatrical reality. I was amazed when I learned that the main rôle was being played by the working man Prokhor, a former soldier. Next day, with pencil and paper in hand, I penetrated into the servants' quarters after dinner, and besought Czar Maximilian to dictate his monologues to me. Prokhor was none too willing, but I clung to him, begged, demanded, implored, gave him no peace. Finally we made ourselves comfortable at the window, and I began to record, using the scratched window-sill as a table, the rhymed speech of Czar Maximilian. Five minutes had scarcely passed when my father appeared at the door, took in the scene at the window and sternly said: "Lyova, to your room!" Inconsolable, I cried on the divan all afternoon.

I composed verses, feeble lines which perhaps showed my early love for words but certainly forecast no poetical future. My elder sister knew of my verses, through her my mother knew, and through my mother, my father. They would ask me to read my verses aloud before guests. It was painfully embarrassing. I would refuse. They would urge me, at first gently, then with irritation, finally with threats. Sometimes I would run away, but my elders knew how to get what they wanted. With a pounding heart, with tears in my eyes, I would read my verses, ashamed of my borrowed lines and limping rhymes.

Be that as it may, I had tasted of the tree of knowledge. Life was unfolding, not merely daily but even hourly. From the torn divan in the dining-room threads stretched to other worlds. Reading opened a new era in my life.

CHAPTER III

ODESSA: MY FAMILY AND MY SCHOOL

IN 1888, great events began to take place in my life: I was sent off to Odessa to study. It happened this way: My mother's nephew, Moissey Filippovich Schpentzer, a man of about twenty-eight, spent a summer in our village. He was a fine and intelligent person who for a minor political offense had been barred from the university on his graduation from high school. He was a bit of a journalist and a bit of a statistician. He came out to the country to fight off tuberculosis. Monya, as he was called, was the pride of his mother and of his several sisters, both because of his abilities and because of his fine character. My family inherited this respect for him. Everybody was pleased at the prospect of his arrival. Quietly I shared this feeling. When Monya entered the dining-room I was at the threshold of the so-called "nursery" —a tiny corner room—and did not have enough courage to come forward because my shoes had two gaping holes. This was not due to poverty—the family at the time was already well-to-do—but to the indifference of country folk, to overburdening toil, to the low level of our home standards.

"Hello, boy," said Moissey Filippovich, "come here."

"Hello," the boy answered, but did not budge from his place. They explained to the guest, with a guilty laugh, why I did not stir. He gaily relieved me of my embarrassment by lifting me across the threshold and embracing me heartily.

Monya was the centre of attention at dinner. Mother served him the best cuts, asking how he enjoyed his food and what his favorite dishes were. In the evening, after the herd had been driven into the cowpen, Monya said to me: "Come on, let's get some fresh milk. Take along some glasses. . . . Now darling, you should hold the glasses with your fingers on the outside, not on the inside."

From Monya I learned many things I did not know: how to hold a glass, how to wash, how to pronounce certain words, and why milk fresh from the cow is good for the chest. He walked a lot, he wrote, he played ninepins, he taught me arithmetic and Russian grammar, preparing me for the first class of the *gymnasium*. He enraptured me but at the same time disquieted me. One sensed in him the element of a more exacting discipline in life—the element of city civilization.

Monya was friendly to his country relatives. He jested a lot and sometimes hummed in a soft tenor voice. At times he seemed gloomy and at the dinner-table would sit silent, sunk in meditation. He would get anxious glances and would be asked if something ailed him. His answers were brief and evasive. Only toward the end of his stay in the village, and then only vaguely, did I begin to surmise the cause of his moody spells. Monya was upset by the rude manners of the village, by some injustice. It was not that his uncle or aunt were especially stern masters—that cannot be said under any circumstances. The nature of the prevailing relations with the laborers and peasants was in no sense worse than on other estates. But it was not much better—and this means that it was oppressive. When the overseer once struck a shepherd with a long knout because he had kept the horses out late, Monya grew pale and hissed between his teeth, "How shameful!" And I felt that it was shameful. I do not know if I would have felt the same way if he had not made his remark—I am inclined to think I would. But in any event he helped me to feel that way, and this alone was enough to instil in me a lifelong sense of gratitude.

Schpentzer was about to marry the principal of the State School for Jewish Girls. No one in Yanovka knew her, but everybody assumed that she must be out of the ordinary, because she was a school principal and Monya's bride. It was decided to send me to Odessa the following spring; there I would live with the Schpentzers and attend the *gymnasium*. The tailor of the colony somehow fitted me out. A large trunk was packed with vessels containing butter, jars full of jam and other gifts for the city relatives. The farewell was a long one. I wept copiously, so did my mother, and so did my sisters, and for the first time I felt how dear to me was Yanovka, with all it held. We drove to the station across the steppe, and I wept until we came out on the main road.

From Novy Bug we took the train to Nikolayev, where we transferred to a steamboat. The siren sent shivers down my spine; it sounded like the call to a new life. The sea was ahead of us, for we were still on the River Bug. A great deal indeed was ahead. There was the pier, the cabman, the Pokrovsky Alley, and a big old house where the School for Girls and its principal were lodged. I was scrutinized from every angle. First a young woman, then an older one—her mother—kissed me on the forehead and both cheeks. Moissey Filippovich jested in his usual manner, inquiring about Yanovka, its inhabitants, and even the familiar cows. To me the cows seemed such insignificant beings that I was embarrassed to discuss them in such select company. The apartment was none too large. I was assigned a corner in the dining-room, behind a curtain. And it was here that I spent the first four years of my school life.

All at once I found myself in the grip of that alluring but exacting discipline which Moissey Filippovich radiated when he was with us in the country. The régime was not stern but it was regular; it was on that account that it seemed severe in the beginning. I had to go to bed at nine. This hour gradually receded as I advanced in the school. I was reminded at every turn not to fail to say good-morning, to keep my hands and finger-nails tidy, not to eat with a knife, not to be tardy, always to thank the servants, and not to speak ill of people behind their backs. I learned that scores of words which seemed beyond question at home were not Russian but Ukrainian jargon. Every day there was revealed to me some aspect of a cultural environment greater than that in which I had passed the first nine years of my life. Even the shop at home began to dim and to lose its magic as compared with the spell of classical literature and the charm of the theatre. I was becoming a little urbanite. Occasionally, however, the village would flare up in my consciousness and draw me on like a lost paradise. Then I would pine, wander about, and trace with my finger on the window-pane messages to my mother, or I would cry into my pillow.

Life in the home of Moissey Filippovich was modest. He had barely means enough to make ends meet. The head of the family had no steady work. He did translations of the Greek tragedies with commentaries, he wrote tales for children, he studied Schloesser and other historians, planning to compile graphic chronological tables, and he helped his wife to conduct the school. It was later that he formed a small publishing house which grew with difficulty in the first years but rose to a high position subsequently. In about ten or twelve years he became the outstanding publisher in southern Russia, the owner of a large printing establishment and of a private residence. I lived for six years with this family, during the first period of the publishing concern. I became very familiar with type, make-up, lay-out, printing, paging, and binding. Proofreading was my favorite pastime. My love for the freshly printed page has its origin in those far-away years as a schoolboy.

As would be the case in bourgeois, especially petty bourgeois, homes, the servant occupied not a small although not a noticeable rôle in my life. The first maid, Dasha, made me her secret confidant, entrusting her various secrets to me. After dinner, when everybody was resting, I would stealthily make for the kitchen. There Dasha would give me fragrants of her life and tell me of her first love. Dasha was followed by a divorced Jewess from Jitomir. "What a rascal he was," she would complain of her former husband. I began to teach her how to read. Every day she would spend not less than half an hour at my desk, trying to penetrate into the mystery of the alphabet and the formation of words. By this time there was an infant in the family, and a wet-nurse was taken in. I wrote letters for her. She complained of her troubles to her husband, who was in America. At her request I painted them in the darkest colors, adding that "our baby is the only bright star on the dark skyline of my life." The nurse was in ecstasy. I myself reread the letter aloud with some satisfaction, although the closing part, where there was something about sending dollars, embarrassed me. Then she added:

"And now, one more letter."

"To whom?" I asked, preparing for the creative task.

"To my cousin," replied the nurse somewhat uncertainly. This letter also spoke of her dark life, but said nothing about the star, and ended with a suggestion that she visit him if he so desired. Hardly had the nurse left with the letters when my pupil, the maid, who had apparently been eavesdropping, appeared. "But he isn't at all a cousin of hers," she whispered to me indignantly. "What is he then?" I asked. "Just somebody," she replied. And I had occasion to contemplate the complexity of human relations.

At dinner Fanny Solomonovna* said to me, smiling strangely: "How about some more soup, author?"

"What?" I asked, alarmed.

"Oh nothing, you composed a letter for the wet-nurse, so you are an author. How did you put it: a star on the dark sky-line?—an author, indeed!" And no longer able to restrain herself, she burst out laughing.

"It's well written," said Moissey Filippovich soothingly, "but you know, you shouldn't write letters for her any more; let Fanny herself write them."

The bewildering wrong side of life, recognized neither at home nor at school, did not however cease to exist because of that, and proved sufficiently powerful and all-pervading to command attention even from a ten-year-old boy. Barred from the schoolroom as well as from the front door of the home, it found its way in through the kitchen.

The law limiting the admission of Jews to the state schools to ten per cent of the entire number was first introduced in 1887. It was an almost hopeless effort to gain entrance into a *gymnasium*, requiring "pull" or bribery. The *realschule* differed from the *gymnasium* in the absence from its curriculum of ancient languages and in its broader course in mathematics, natural sciences and modern languages. The ten per cent statute applied also to the *realschule*. In the case of the latter, the stream of applicants was smaller and the chances for admission were therefore greater. For a long time a debate raged in the newspapers and magazines as to the merits of a classical *vs.* a *realschule* education. The conservatives held that classicism fosters discipline—it was more likely a hope that the citizen who had endured Greek in his childhood would be able to endure the Czarist régime the rest of his life. The liberals, on the other hand, without repudiating classicism, which is a sort of a foster-brother to liberalism, since both trace their origin to the Renaissance, still favored the *realschule*. When I

* The wife of Moissey Filippovich.

45

was about to start my high-school education, these debates had died down, the result of a special order prohibiting discussion as to which was the more desirable type of education.

In the fall, I took my examinations for the first class of the St. Paul *realschule.* . I passed the entrance examination with average marks: a "3" in Russian, a "4" in arithmetic.* This was not enough, as the ten per cent statute meant the most rigid selection—complicated, of course, by bribery. It was decided to put me in the preparatory class, attached to the school as a private institution. Jews were transferred from there to the first class according to the statute, it is true, but with preference over outsiders.

The St. Paul School had originally `en a German institution. It had been founded by the L `neran parish to serve the numerous German residents of ` dessa and of the southern district in general. Although t` St. Paul School was endowed with all state rights, it wa` ecessary, because it had only six grades, to take the sever`. year at another *realschule* in order to be admitted to a uni`ersity. Apparently the assumption was that in the last grade the remnants of the German spirit would be wiped out. This spirit, by the way, waned in the St. Paul School year by year. Germans formed less than half of the student body. The Germans on the staff were persistently being forced out.

The first days of study at school were days of sorrow; then they became days of joy. I started for school in a brand-new uniform, wearing a new cap with a yellow border and a remarkable metal badge which contained, between two trefoils, the complicated monogram of the school. On my back was a brand-new leather school-bag, holding new text-books in bright bindings and a handsome pencil-case stuffed with freshly sharpened pencils, a new penholder, and an eraser. In transports, I carried this entire, magnificent load through the long Uspensky Street, happy that the distance to the school was great. It seemed to me that the passers-by looked with amazement and sometimes even with envy at my astonishing equipment. Trustingly and with interest I surveyed everybody I

* In the Russian system of grading, "5" was the highest and "1" the lowest mark.—*Translator.*

46

met. Then, quite suddenly, a tall skinny boy of about thirteen, evidently a shop-apprentice, for he carried some tin object, stopped in front of this superb schoolboy and coming within a step or two, threw his head back, made a loud noise and spat amply at the shoulder of my new jacket. Looking contemptuously at me, he passed on without a word. What made him do it? I know the reason now. The impoverished boy, dressed in a tattered shirt, with broken boots on bare feet, the boy whose job it was to carry out the dirty errands of his masters while their pampered sons flaunted school uniforms, vented upon me his sense of social protest. But at the time I was not interested in generalities. I wiped my shoulder for a long time with some leaves, boiling within from the helpless insult, and completed the last part of my journey in a gloomy mood.

The second blow awaited me in the courtyard of the school. "Peter Pavlovich," the boys cried, "here is another from the preparatory class in uniform!" What did that mean? It appeared that the preparatory school was a private affair, and its members were strictly forbidden to don the St. Paul uniform. Peter Pavlovich, the black-bearded monitor, explained to me that I must remove the badge, the braid and the belt-buckle, and must replace the buttons, which had an eagle stamped on them, with ordinary ones. This was my second misfortune.

That day there were no classes at school. The German pupils and many others were all gathered in the Lutheran church whose name the school bore. I found myself under the guidance of a thick-set boy who had been left in the preparatory class for a second year and who knew the system. He put me next to him on a bench at the church. For the first time I heard an organ, and its sounds filled me with quivers. Then appeared a tall, shaven man, the facing of his coat all white; his voice reverberated through the church like a series of waves. The strangeness of his speech accentuated tenfold the grandeur of his sermon. "Who is that speaking?" I asked, all agitated. "It's Pastor Binneman himself," explained my new friend, Carlson. "He's a terribly wise man, the wisest in Odessa."

"And what is he saying?"

"Well, you know, the regular things," said Carlson with much less enthusiasm. "That one should be a good pupil, study

47

hard, get along well with the boys." This heavy-jawed ad-
mirer of Binneman turned out to be a most obstinate sluggard
and a terrible scrapper who, during recesses, distributed black
eyes right and left.

The second day brought its comforts. I promptly distinguished myself in arithmetic, and copied the lesson from the
blackboard well. The teacher, Rudyenko, praised me before the
entire class and gave me two "fives." This reconciled me to the
plain buttons on my jacket. The director himself, Christian
Christianovich Schwannebach, taught German to the junior
classes. He was a sleek official who had attained his high position only because he was the brother-in-law of Binneman
himself. Christian Christianovitch began by examining the
hands of all the pupils. He found that mine were clean. Then,
when I had copied his lesson from the blackboard accurately,
the director voiced his approval and gave me a "5." Thus it
came about that after the first actual day of school I was returning with a load of three "excellent" marks. I carried
them in my leather kit like a treasure, and ran rather than
walked into the Pokrovsky Alley, driven by the thirst for home
glory.

So I became a schoolboy. I would rise early, drink my
morning tea in a hurry, thrust a package containing my lunch
into my overcoat pocket, and run to school in order to reach
there in time for the morning prayer. I was not tardy. I was
quiet at my desk. I listened attentively and copied carefully.
I worked diligently at home over my lessons. I went to bed at
the prescribed hour, in order to hurry through my tea the following morning and run to school for fear of being late for
the prayer. I passed from grade to grade without difficulty.
Whenever I met one of my teachers in the street, I bowed with
all possible deference.

The percentage of freaks among people in general is very
considerable, but it is especially high among teachers. In the
St. Paul *realschule* the level of the teachers was perhaps above
the average. The standing of the school was high, and not
without reason. The régime was stern and exacting; the reins
were drawn tighter and tighter every year, especially after the
director's power had passed from the hands of Schwannebach
into those of Nikolay Antonovich Kaminsky. He was a phys-

icist by profession, a humanity-hater by temperament. He never looked at the person with whom he talked; he moved about the corridors and the classrooms noiselessly on rubber heels. He spoke in a small, hoarse, falsetto voice which, without being raised, could be terrifying. Outwardly Kaminsky seemed even in temper, but inwardly he was always in a state of habitual irritation. His attitude toward even the best students was one of armed neutrality. That, incidentally, was his attitude toward me.

In his capacity of physicist, Kaminsky invented a special apparatus to demonstrate the Boyle-Mariotte law of the resistance of gases. After each demonstration, there were always two or three boys who in a studied whisper would exchange the words, "Well done!" Some one would rise and in a doubtful tone inquire: "And who is the inventor of this apparatus?" Kaminsky would answer casually in his frozen falsetto: "I built it." Everybody would exchange glances, and the two-mark boys would emit as loud a sigh of rapture as possible.

After Schwannebach had been replaced by Kaminsky as a measure for Russification, the teacher of literature, Anton Vasilyevich Krizhanovsky, became the inspector of the school. He was a red-bearded, crafty fellow, an ex-theologian, a great lover of gifts—a man with a slightly liberal tendency, very clever at disguising his designs under an assumed kindliness. As soon as he was appointed inspector he became more rigorous and conservative. Krizhanovsky taught Russian from the first grade upward. He singled me out for my grammar and love of the language. He made it a fixed rule to read my written works aloud to the class, giving me a mark of "5 plus."

The mathematician, Yurchenko, was a stubby, phlegmatic, shrewd person, who was known as the "bindyuzhnik," which in Odessa slang meant a "heavy truck-driver." Yurchenko addressed everybody, from the first grade to the last, by the familiar "thou," and was not finicky about his expressions. With his consistent gruffness, he inspired a certain amount of respect which melted away, however, in the course of time, for the boys learned that Yurchenko took bribes. The other teachers were also susceptible to bribery in one form or another. A backward pupil, if he was from out of town, would be lodged with that teacher whom he needed most. If the pupil happened to be a local resident, he would employ the threatening pedagogue as a private tutor at a high price.

The second mathematician, Zlotchansky, was the opposite of Yurchenko. He was thin, with a prickly mustache on a greenish-yellow face; his eyeballs were muddy, his movements as sluggish as if he had just awakened. He coughed noisily and spat in the classroom. It was known that he had had an unhappy love-affair, that he was dissipating and drinking. Although not a bad mathematician, Zlotchansky would stare beyond his pupils, beyond his studies, and even beyond his mathematics. Several years later he cut his throat with a razor.

My relations with the two mathematicians were smooth and pleasant, since I was strong in the subject. When I was in the last grades of the *realschule*, I planned to go in for higher mathematics.

The teacher of history was Lyubimov, a large and imposing man with gold-rimmed glasses on a small nose, and with a manly young beard around his full face. Only when he smiled did it suddenly appear, clearly even to us boys, that the impressiveness of the man was superficial, that he was weak-willed, timid, torn within himself, and fearful lest people find out something about him.

I plunged into history with an increasing though diffused interest. Gradually I widened the circle of my studies, abandoning the poor official text-books for the university courses or the solid tomes of Schloesser. There was undoubtedly some element of sport in my fascination for history. I learned by heart many unnecessary names and details, burdensome to the memory, in order to give occasional embarrassment to the teacher. Lyubimov was unable to cope with his class. Sometimes he would suddenly flare up during the lesson and look angrily about, catching a whisper that he imagined to be an insulting remark concerning himself. The class would prick up its ears in astonishment. Lyubimov also taught at a *gymnasium* for girls, and there, too, it was observed that he was acting strangely. The end was an attack of insanity, as a result of which Lyubimov hanged himself from a window-frame.

The geography teacher, Zhukovsky, was feared more than fire. He mowed the boys down like an automatic meat-axe. Zhukovsky demanded an entirely impossible silence in his classroom. Not infrequently stopping a student in the midst of his recitation, he would look up sharply like a bird of prey listening to the sound of distant danger. Everybody knew what it meant: not to stir and if possible not to breathe. I recall only one occasion when Zhukovsky loosed his reins somewhat. I think it was on his birthday. One of the students said something to him that was semi-private, that is, with no bearing on the lesson. Zhukovsky tolerated it. This in itself was an event. Immediately Vakker, the fawner, arose and, with a smirk, remarked: "It's common talk that Lyubimov can't hold a candle to Zhukovsky." Zhukovsky suddenly grew tense. "What's that? Sit down!" At once there descended that special silence known only in the geography class. Vakker sat down as if crushed by a blow. Glances full of reproach and disgust were turned upon him from all sides. "I swear, it's the truth," Vakker replied in a whisper, hoping to touch the heart of the geographer, with whom his standing was low.

The full-fledged teacher of German at the school was Struve, a huge German with a large head and a beard which reached to his waist-line. This man carried his heavy body, which seemed a vessel of kindliness, on almost childlike limbs. Struve was a most honest person; he suffered over the failures of his pupils, he shared their agitation, he coaxed them, and was pained over every "2." He never descended as low as a "1"; he tried never to leave a pupil behind for another year. It was he who had obtained admission to the school for the nephew of his cook, the Vakker boy, who turned out, however, to be ungifted and unattractive. Struve was a bit droll, but on the whole a sympathetic figure.

The teacher of French was Gustave Samoylovich Burnande, a Swiss—a lean person with a profile so flat that it seemed to have just been squeezed in a press. He had a small bald spot, thin, blue, unkindly lips, a sharp nose, and a mysterious large scar in the form of the letter X on his forehead. Burnande was disliked unanimously, and with reason. A sufferer from indigestion, he kept swallowing tablets during the classroom hours, and regarded every pupil as a personal enemy. The scar on his forehead was a constant source of conjecture and theory. It was said that Gustave in his youth had fought a duel, and that his opponent succeeded in tracing a twisted cross on his forehead with a rapier. This was denied several months later. It was then asserted that there had been no duel but instead a surgical operation, in the course of which part of his forehead was employed to repair his nose. The boys carefully scrutinized his nose, and the more venturesome ones affirmed that they could see the stitches. Then there were more judicial minds who sought to explain the scar as an accident of his early childhood—a fall down stairs. But this explanation was repudiated as too prosaic. Moreover, it was altogether impossible to imagine Burnande as a child.

The chief janitor, who played a not unimportant rôle in our life, was the imperturbable German Anton, with imposing and graying side-whiskers. When it came to tardiness, being kept after school, incarceration, Anton's authority was merely a routine affair, but actually it was great, and it was necessary to keep on friendly terms with him. My attitude toward him was one of indifference, as was his toward me, for I was not among his clients. I came to school on time, my kit was in order, my card was always in the left pocket of my jacket. But scores of pupils were daily at the mercy of Anton and courted his benevolence in every way. In any event, he was for all of us one of the pillars of the St. Paul *realschule*. Imagine our amazement when, on our return from the summer vacation, we learned that old man Anton had shot the eighteen-year-old daughter of another janitor in a fit of passion and jealousy, and was lodged in jail.

In this way the regulated life of the school and the suppressed, crushed public life of the period would be punctured by individual personal calamities which always made an exaggerated impression, like a sob in an empty vault.

There was an orphanage attached to the church of St. Paul. It occupied a corner of our courtyard. Dressed in blue, washworn denim, the inmates appeared in the yard with unhappy faces, wandering dejectedly in their corner and droopingly climbing the stairs. In spite of the fact that the courtyard was common ground and the orphanage not segregated, the schoolboys and the inmates represented two completely separate worlds. Once or twice I tried to converse with the boys in blue denim, but they answered gruffly, unwillingly, hurrying to their own section. They were under strict orders not to interfere in the affairs of the students. For seven years I played in this courtyard, and never knew the name of a single orphan. One must suppose that Pastor Binneman blessed them at the beginning of the year, according to the abbreviated mass-book.

In the part of the courtyard which adjoined the orphanage was the complicated apparatus for gymnastics: rings, poles, ladders—both vertical and inclined—trapezes, parallel bars, et cetera. Soon after I entered school, I wanted to repeat a stunt performed before me by one of the orphanage boys. Climbing the vertical ladder and suspending myself by my shoe-tips from the upper bar, head downward, I caught the lowest rung within reach and, releasing my feet, let myself go, expecting to make a loop of 180 degrees and land on the ground in one bound. But I failed to let go my hands in time and, after describing the loop, struck the ladder with my body. My chest was crushed, my breath stifled; I wriggled on the ground like a worm, grasping at the legs of the boys around me, and then losing consciousness. From then on I was more careful with my gymnastics.

My life was not of the street, of the market-place, of sports and outdoor exercises. I made up for these deficiencies when on vacation in the village. The city seemed to me created for study and reading. The boys' street brawls seemed to me disgraceful. Yet there was never any lack of cause for a fight.

The *gymnasium* students, on account of their silver buttons and badges, were dubbed "herrings," while the brass-buttoned *realschule* boys were called "kippers." Returning home along the Yamskaya, I was accosted once by a long-bodied *gymnasium* student who kept asking: "What do you charge for kippers?" Getting no answer to his question, he shoved me along with his shoulder. "What do you want of me?" I asked in a tone of extreme courtesy. The student was taken ab ck.

He hesitated for a moment and then asked:

"Have you got a sling-shot?"

"A sling-shot," I asked in turn, "what's that?"

The long-bodied student silently pulled out of his ket a small apparatus consisting of a rubber band on a pro stick, and a piece of lead. "From the window I kill ons on the roof, and then fry them," he said. I looked at new ac-

quaintance with surprise. Such an occupation was not unin-
viting, but it seemed nevertheless somewhat out of place and
almost indecent in city surroundings.

Many of the boys went boating on the sea, many fished from
the breakwater. These pleasures I did not know. Strangely
enough, the sea had no part in my life in that period, although
I spent seven years on its shores. During all that time I never
was in a boat at sea, never fished, and generally encountered
the sea only during my trips to the village and back. When
Carlson showed up on Monday with a sunburned nose from
which the skin was peeling, and boasted of catching chubs from
a boat, his joys seemed remote and did not touch me at all.
The passionate hunter and fisherman in me had not yet awakened in those days.

While in the preparatory class I became very chummy with
Kostya R., the son of a physician. Kostya was one year
younger than I, smaller in size, quiet in appearance, but actually a scapegrace and a rogue, with keen little eyes. He knew
the town well and in this respect had a great advantage over me.
He did not excel in his studies, whereas I had from the beginning maintained a record of the highest marks. At home
Kostya did nothing but talk of his new friend. The result was
that his mother, a little, dried-up woman, came to Fanny Solomonovna with the request that the two boys study together.
After the conference, in which I participated, permission was
granted. For two or three years we occupied the same bench.
Then Kostya was left a grade behind, and we parted. Our relations, however, continued in later years.

Kostya had a sister in the *gymnasium* about two years his
senior. The sister had girl friends. These friends had brothers. The girls studied music. The boys hung around their
sisters' friends. On birthdays the parents invited guests.
There was a little world of sympathies, jealousies, dancing,
games, envies, and animosities. The centre of this little world
was the family of the wealthy merchant A., who occupied an
apartment in the same house and on the same floor where Kostya lived. The corridors of the apartments all faced the same
balcony in the courtyard. It was on the balcony that all sorts
of meetings took place, casual and otherwise. In the home of
A. there was an atmosphere altogether different from the one

to which I had grown accustomed at the Schpentzers'. Here were many schoolboys and schoolgirls practising the art of flirtation under the patronizing smile of the mistress of the house. In the course of conversation, it would crop out who was interested in whom. For such matters I always displayed the greatest contempt, which was, however, a bit hypocritical. "When you fall in love with any one," the fourteen-year-old daughter of A. would instruct me, "you must tell me."

"I can promise you that, since I am in no danger of doing it," I would answer with the assumed pride of a man who knows his value—I was then already in the second grade. A couple of weeks later the girls gave an exhibition of *tableaux vivants*. The younger daughter, with her hands raised, represented Night, against the background of a large black shawl sprinkled with stars made from silver paper.

"Look how pretty she is," remarked the older sister, nudging me. I looked, agreed in my heart, and right there and then made a decision: the hour had come to fulfil the promise. Soon the older sister began to question me. "Have you nothing to tell me?" Dropping my eyes, I replied: "I have."

"Who is she, then?"

But my tongue would not move. She proposed that I give the first letter of her name. This made it easier. The name of the older girl was Anna. The younger sister was named Bertha. I gave the second letter of the alphabet, and not the first.

"B?" she repeated, obviously disappointed, and there the conversation ended.

The following day, I was on my way to Kostya to study, walking as usual through the long corridor of the third floor. From the staircase, I had already observed that the two sisters were sitting on the balcony with their mother. When I was within a few feet of the group, I felt myself pierced by their needlelike glances of irony. The younger girl did not smile, but on the contrary looked away from me, her face wearing an expression of terrifying indifference. This convinced me at once that I had been betrayed. The mother and the older girl shook hands with me in a manner which clearly said: "Fine gosling, now we know what is underneath your seriousness." The younger sister stretched out her hand, flat as a little board,

without looking at me and without answering my handclasp.
I still had quite a walk along the balcony to negotiate, in full
sight of my tormentors. All the time I felt their murderous
arrows in my back. After that unheard-of treachery, I decided
to sever my relations completely with this perfidious clan, not
to call on them, to forget them, tear them out of my heart forever. I was helped by the vacation period, which came soon
afterward.

Unexpectedly for me, it appeared that I was near-sighted.
I was taken to an eye-specialist, who supplied me with glasses.
This did not hurt my pride at all, for the glasses gave me a
sense of added importance. Not without some satisfaction did
I anticipate my appearance in Yanovka wearing glasses. For
my father, however, the glasses were a great blow. He held
that it was affectation and swank on my part, and peremp-
torily demanded that I remove them. In vain did I protest that
I could not read the writing on the blackboard and the signs
on the streets. In Yanovka I wore the glasses only secretly.

And yet, in the country I was much more courageous and
enterprising, and showed more abandon. I shook off the discipline of the city. I would go to Bobrinetz on horseback all
alone, and return the same day toward evening. This was a
journey of fifty kilometres. In Bobrinetz I displayed my
glasses publicly and had no doubt as to the impression they
made. There was but one municipal boys' school in Bobrinetz.
The nearest *gymnasium* was in Elizavetgrad, fifty kilometres
away. There was a junior girls' high school in Bobrinetz, and
during the school season the girls recruited their friends from
among the students of the municipal school. In the summer
things were different. The high-school boys would return
from Elizavetgrad, and the magnificence of their uniforms and
the finesse of their manners would push the municipal pupils
into the background. The antagonism was bitter. The offended
Bobrinetz schoolboys would form fighting groups and on occasion would resort not only to sticks and stones but to knives
as well. As I was sitting nonchalantly eating berries on the
branch of a mulberry-tree in the garden of some friends, some
one threw a stone at me from behind a fence, hitting me on
the head. This was but one small incident in a long and not
entirely bloodless warfare, interrupted only by the departure

of the privileged class from Bobrinetz. Things were different in Elizavetgrad. There the high-school students dominated both streets and hearts. In the summer, however, the university students would arrive from Kharkoff, Odessa and more distant cities, and shove the high-school boys into their backyards. Here the struggle was likewise fierce, and the perfidy of the girls was indescribable. But the fight, as a rule, was waged only with spiritual or moral weapons.

In the country I played croquet and ninepins, led in forfeits, and was insolent to the girls. It was there that I learned to ride a bicycle made entirely by Ivan Vasilyevich. Because of that, I dared later to exercise on the Odessa track. In the village, moreover, I managed all alone a blooded stallion in a two-wheeled gig. By this time there were already fine driving-horses in Yanovka. I offered to take my uncle Brodsky, the brewer, for a ride. "I won't be thrown out?" asked my uncle, who was not inclined to daring enterprise. "How can you, uncle?" I replied, so indignantly that with a meek sigh he sat down behind me. I made for the ravine and passed the mill, going along a road fresh from a summer rain. The bay stallion was seeking the open spaces, and, irritated by the necessity of going up-hill, suddenly tore ahead. I pulled on the reins, pushing against the foot-bar, and raised myself high enough so that my uncle could not see that I was hanging onto the reins. But the stallion had his mind made up. He was three times younger than I—only four years old. Annoyed, he pulled the gig up the hill like a cat trying to run away from a tin can tied to its tail. I began to sense that my uncle had stopped smoking behind me, that he was breathing faster and was about to issue an ultimatum. I settled down more solidly, loosening the reins on the bay stallion, and to appear fully confident, I clicked my tongue in time with the spleen, which was pounding beautifully in the bay. "Now don't you play, boy," I admonished him patronizingly when he tried to gallop. I spread my arms more at ease and felt that my uncle had calmed down and had taken up his cigarette again. The game was won, although my heart was beating like the spleen of the horse.

Returning to town, I again bent my neck to the yoke of discipline. It was no great effort. Exercises and sports gave way to books and occasionally the theatre. I surrendered to the city, but hardly came in contact with it. Its life almost passed by me. And not by me alone—even the grown-ups dared not stick their heads too far out the windows. Odessa was perhaps the most police-ridden city in police-ridden Russia. The main personage in town was the governor, the former Admiral Zelenoy 2d. He combined absolute power with an uncurbed temper. Innumerable anecdotes, which the Odessites exchanged in whispers, circulated about him. At that time there appeared abroad, printed in a free plant, a whole book of tales of the heroic deeds of Admiral Zelenoy 2d. I saw him but once, and then only his back. But that was enough for me. The governor was standing in his carriage, fully erect, and was cursing in his throaty voice across the street, shaking his fist. Policemen with their hands at attention and janitors with their caps in hand passed by him in review, and from behind curtained windows frightened faces looked out. I adjusted my school kit and hurried home.

Whenever I want to restore in my memory the scene of official Russia in the years of my early youth, I visualize the back of that governor, his fist stretched into space, and I hear his throaty curses, not usually found in dictionaries.

CHAPTER IV

BOOKS AND EARLY CONFLICTS

In my inner life, not only during my school years but throughout my youth, nature and individuals occupied a lesser place than books and ideas. Despite my country bringing-up, I was not sensitive to nature. My interest in it and my understanding of it came in later years, when childhood and even early youth were far behind. For a long time people passed through my mind like random shadows. I looked into myself and into books, in which in turn I tried again to find myself and my future.

My reading commenced in 1887 after the arrival at Yanovka of Moissey Filippovich, who brought with him a pile of books, including some of Tolstoy's writings for the people. At first reading was more of a task than a pleasure. Every new book brought with it new obstacles, such as unfamiliar words, unintelligible human relationships, and the vagueness and instability which separate fancy from reality. Usually there was nobody at hand to answer my questions, and so I was often at sea—beginning a book, giving it up and beginning it again—joining the uncertain joy of knowledge with the fear of the unknown. One might perhaps liken my reading experiences during that period to a night drive on the steppes: squeaking wheels and voices crossing one another, bonfires along the road flaring up in the darkness; everything seems familiar and yet one does not quite grasp its meaning. What is happening? Who is driving past—and carrying what? Even oneself—where is one going, forward or backward? Nothing is clear, and there is nobody like Uncle Gregory to explain: "These are drivers carrying wheat."

In Odessa the choice of books was vastly greater, and with it went attentive and sympathetic guidance. I devoured books ravenously and had to be forced to go out for walks. On my walks I would live through again in my mind what I had read, and then would hurry home to resume the reading. In the evenings I would beg to be allowed to stay up another quarter of an hour, or even only five minutes to finish the chapter. Hardly an evening passed without an argument of this kind.

The awakened hunger to see, to know, to absorb, found relief in this insatiable swallowing of printed matter,—in the hands and lips of a child ever reaching out for the cup of verbal fancy. Everything in my later life that was interesting or thrilling, gay or sad, was already present in my reading experiences as a hint, a promise, a slight and timid sketch in pencil or water-color.

During the first years of my stay in Odessa, reading aloud in the evenings, after I finished my home work and until I went to bed, gave me my happiest hours, or rather half-hours. Moissey Filippovich usually read Pushkin or Nekrassov, more often the latter. But at the hour set, Fanny Solomonovna would say, "It's time to go to bed, Lyova." I would look at her with imploring eyes. "It's time to sleep, little boy," Moissey Filippovich would say. "Another five minutes," I begged, and the five minutes were granted. After that, I kissed them good-night and went off with the feeling that I could listen to their reading all night, though I had scarcely laid my head on the pillow before I was fast asleep.

A girl in the last grade of high school, a distant relative called Sophia, came to stay with the Schpentzers for a few weeks until her family got over an attack of scarlet fever. She was a very capable and well-read girl, although, since she lacked originality and character, she soon faded away for me. But I admired her tremendously, and every day found in her new stores of knowledge and new qualities; by contrast I appeared in my own eyes as utterly insignificant. I helped her by copying her examination programme, and generally in various other small ways. In return, when the grown-ups were resting after dinner, she would read aloud to me. Before long we began to compose together a satirical poem, "A Journey to the Moon." In this work I always lagged behind. No sooner had I made some modest suggestion than the senior collaborator would catch the idea "on the wing," develop it, introduce variations, and pick up rhymes without effort, what time I was, so to speak, being hauled in tow. When the six weeks were up and Sophia returned to her home, I felt that I had grown older.

Among the more notable friends of the family there was Sergey Ivanovich Sychevsky, an old journalist and a romantic personality, who was known in the South of Russia as an authority on Shakespeare. He was a gifted man but was addicted to drink. Because of this weakness, he wore a guilty air toward people, even toward children. He had known Fanny Solomonovna since her early youth, and called her "Fannyushka." Sergey Ivanovich became attached to me at the very first meeting. After asking what we were studying at school, the old man told me to write a paper comparing Pushkin's "Poet and Bookseller" with Nekrassov's "Poet and Citizen." This nearly took my breath away. I had never even read the second work and, what was still more important, I was intimidated by the fact that Sychevsky was an *author*. The very word "author" sounded to me as if it was uttered from some unattainable height. "We will read it right away," said Sergey Ivanovich, and began instantly to read. He read superbly. "Did you understand? Well, put it all into your essay." They seated me in the study, gave me Pushkin's and Nekrassov's works, paper and ink.

"I tell you, I can't do it," I swore in a tragic whisper to Fanny Solomonovna. "What can I write here?"

"Now, don't you get excited," she answered, stroking my head. "You write just as you understand it—that's all."

Her hand was tender, and so was her voice. I calmed down a little, or rather got my frightened vanity under control, and began to write. About an hour later, I was summoned to show the result. I brought in a large sheet of paper, written all over, and, shaking in my boots as I never did at school, handed it to the "author." Sergey Ivanovich ran over a few lines in silence, and, turning his sparkling eyes to me, exclaimed: "Just listen to what he wrote. He is a smart fellow, I swear!" And then he read: " 'The poet lived with his beloved nature, whose every sound, both gay and sad, echoed in the Poet's heart.' Didn't he word it beautifully, 'whose every sound'—just listen to this—'both gay and sad, echoed in the Poet's heart.' " And so deeply did those words engrave themselves that day on my own mind that I have remembered them ever since.

At dinner, Sergey Ivanovich joked a great deal, delved into memories of the past, and told stories, finding inspiration in

the glass of vodka which was always ready at his call. Now
and again he looked at me across the table and said: "Where
ever did you learn to put it so well? Really, I must give you
a kiss." Then, wiping his mustache carefully with a napkin,
he rose and with unsteady steps set out on a trip around the
table. I sat as if waiting for some catastrophic blow; a glad-
some blow, it is true, but catastrophic all the same. "Go and
meet him, Lyova," Moissey Filippovich whispered to me. After
dinner Sergey Ivanovich recited from memory the satirical
"Popóv's Dream." Tensely I watched his gray mustache, from
under which there escaped such funny words. The author's
half-drunken state did not in the least impair his eminence in
my eyes. Children possess a remarkable power of abstraction.

In the evenings before it was dark I sometimes went for
walks with Moissey Filippovich, and when he was in a good
humor we talked about all sorts of things. On one occasion he
told me the story of the opera "Faust," which he liked very
much. As I eagerly followed the story, I hoped that one day
I might hear the opera on the stage. From a change in his
tone, however, I became aware that the story was approaching a delicate point. I was quite disturbed by his embarrassment and began to fear that I should not hear the end of the
story. But Moissey Filippovich recovered his calm and continued: "Then a baby was born to Gretchen before marriage. . . ." We both felt relieved when we had passed this
point; after that the story was safely brought to its conclusion.

I was in bed with a bandaged throat, and by way of con-
solation was given Dickens' "Oliver Twist." The remark of
the doctor in the nursing home about the woman's not having
a wedding-ring perplexed me utterly.

"What does it mean?" I asked Moissey Filippovich. "What
has the wedding-ring to do with it?"

"Oh," said he, somewhat haltingly, "it is simply that when
people are not married, they wear no wedding-ring."

I recalled Gretchen. And the fate of Oliver Twist was spun
out in my imagination from a ring, a ring which did not exist.
The forbidden world of human relations burst into my consciousness fitfully from books, and much that I had heard
spoken of in a casual, and usually coarse and gross manner,
now through literature became generalized and ennobled, rising
to some higher plane.

At that time, public opinion was stirred up over Tolstoy's "Power of Darkness," which had just appeared. People discussed it with great earnestness and were unable to come to any definite conclusion. Pobedonostzev succeeded in inducing Czar Alexander III to prohibit the play from being performed. I knew that Moissey Filippovich and Fanny Solomonovna, after I had gone to bed, read the play in the adjoining room. I could hear the murmur of their voices. "May I read it, too?" I asked. "No, dear, you are too young for that," came the answer, and it sounded so categorical that I made no attempt to argue. At the same time I noticed that the slim new volume found its way to the familiar book-shelf. Seizing an opportunity when my guardians were out, I read Tolstoy's play in a few hurried instalments. It impressed me much less vividly than my mentors apparently feared it would. The most tragic scenes, such as the strangling of the child and the conversation about the creaking bones, were accepted not as a terrible reality, but as a literary invention, a stage trick; in other words, I did not really grasp them at all.

During a vacation in the country, while I was exploring a book-shelf high up under the ceiling, I came across a booklet brought home from Elizavetgrad by my elder brother. I opened it and instantly sensed something extraordinary and secret. This was a court report of a murder case in which a little girl was the victim of a sexual crime. I read the book, strewn with medical and legal details, with my mind all astir and alarmed, as if I had found myself in a wood at night, stumbling against ghostlike, moonlit trees and not able to find my way out. Human psychology, particularly in the case of children, has its own buffers, brakes, and safety-valves—an extensive and well-devised system which stands guard against untimely and too drastic shocks.

My first visit to the theatre took place when I was in the preparatory class at school. It was like no other experience, and beggars description. I was sent, under the chaperonage of the school janitor, Gregory Kholod, to see a Ukrainian play. I sat pale as a sheet—so Gregory afterward reported to Fanny Solomonovna—and was tortured by a joy which was more than I could bear. During the intermissions I did not leave my seat, lest—God forbid!—I might miss something. The performance ended with a comic sketch: "A Tenant with a Trombone." The tension of drama was now relieved by riotous laughter. I swayed in my seat, now throwing back my head, and now again riveting my eyes on the stage. At home I related the story of the tenant with a trombone, adding more and more details every time, hoping to arouse the laughter which I had just experienced. To my great disappointment, I found my efforts quite wasted. "It seems you did not like the 'Nazar Stodolya' at all—did you?" asked Moissey Filippovich. I felt these words as an inner reproach. I thought of Nazar's sufferings and said: "No, it was quite remarkable."

Before passing to the third grade, I lived for a short time outside Odessa in the summer home of my engineer uncle. There I attended an amateur theatrical in which a boy from our school, Kruglyakov, played the part of a servant. Kruglyakov was a weak-chested, freckled boy, with intelligent eyes, but in a very poor state of health. I became greatly attached to him and begged him to stage some play with me. We chose Pushkin's "The Niggardly Knight." I had to act the rôle of the son, and Kruglyakov that of the father. I unreservedly accepted his guidance, and spent whole days learning Pushkin's lines. What delicious excitement this was! Soon, however, everything went to pieces: Kruglyakov's parents vetoed his participation in the theatrical on account of his health. When school opened again, he attended classes only the first few weeks. I always tried to catch him after school so that I could engage him in literary conversation on the way home. Soon after that, Kruglyakov disappeared altogether. I learned that he was ill. A few months later came the report that he had died of consumption.

The magic of the theatre held its spell over me for several years. Later I developed a fondness for Italian opera, which was the pride of Odessa. In the sixth grade I even did some tutoring to earn money for the theatre. For several months I was mutely in love with the coloratura soprano bearing the mysterious name of Giuseppina Uget, who seemed to me to have descended from heaven to the stage-boards of the Odessa theatre.

I was not supposed to read newspapers. But the rule was not very strictly observed, and gradually, with a few setbacks, I won the right to read papers, more particularly the feuilleton columns. The centre of interest in the press of Odessa was occupied by the theatre, especially the opera, and such public divisions of opinion as occurred were mainly inspired by theatrical preferences. This was the only sphere in which the newspapers were allowed to display any semblance of temperament.

In those days the star of Doroshevich, the feuilleton-columnist, shone particularly brightly. Within a short time he became the idol of the city, although he wrote of small and, not infrequently, trivial things. But unquestionably he had talent, and by the daring form of his actually innocent articles he let fresh air into an Odessa oppressed to a state of strangulation by the governor, Zelenoy 2d. When I opened the morning paper, I immediately looked for the name of Doroshevich. This enthusiasm for his articles was then shared both by the moderate fathers and by their children who had not yet become immoderate.

From early years my love for words had now been losing now gaining in force, but generally putting down ever firmer roots. In my eyes, authors, journalists, and artists always stood for a world which was more attractive than any other, one open only to the elect.

In the second grade we started a magazine. Moissey Filippovich and I had many talks on this subject, and Moissey Filippovich even devised a title: *The Drop*—the idea being that the second grade of the St. Paul *realschule* was contributing its "drop" to the ocean of literature. I embodied this in a poem which took the place of an introductory article. There were other poems and stories, likewise mostly mine. One of our draftsmen decorated the cover with an involved ornamental design. Somebody suggested showing *The Drop* to Krizha-
——————was undertaken by the boy Y., who lived in —————ny's house. He performed his task with real brilliance: he rose from his seat, walked up to the master's desk, firmly laid *The Drop* upon it, ceremoniously bowed, and returned to his seat. We all held our breath. Krizhanovsky looked at the cover, made a few grimaces with his mustache, eyebrows, and beard, and silently began to read. There was complete quiet in the room; only the leaves of *The Drop* rustled. Then he got up from his desk and with great feeling

read aloud my "Pure little drop." "Good?" he asked. "Good," answered the boys in chorus. "Yes, it may be good, but the author knows nothing about versification. Now, tell me, what is a dactyl?" he turned to me, having guessed the author behind the thinly disguised nom-de-plume. "I don't know," I had to confess. "Then I'll tell you." And neglecting several lessons in grammar and syntax, Krizhanovsky explained to the little second-grade boys the mysteries of metric versification. "And as for the magazine," he said at the end, "it will be better if you don't bother about it or the ocean of literature either, but let this be just your exercise-book." It must be explained that school magazines were forbidden at that time. The question, however, found a different solution. The peaceful course of my studies was suddenly interrupted by my expulsion from the St. Paul *realschule*.

From the days of my childhood I had many conflicts in life, which sprang, as a jurist would say, out of the struggle against injustice. The same motive not infrequently determined my making or breaking of friendships. It would take too long to go through all the numerous episodes. But there were two which assumed considerable proportions.

My biggest conflict occurred in the second grade with Burnande, whom we nicknamed "The Frenchman," though he was really a Swiss. In the school the German language, to some extent, rivalled the Russian. Our French, on the other hand, showed very little progress. Most of the boys learned French for the first time at school, but the German colonists found it particularly difficult. Burnande waged a relentless war against the Germans. His favorite victim was Vakker. The latter was really a very poor scholar. But this time many if not all of us got the impression that the boy did not deserve the lowest marks that Burnande gave him. And that day Burnande was even more ferocious than ever, swallowing a double dose of dyspepsia tablets.

"Let's give him a concert," the boys began whispering around, winking at and nudging one another. Among them I occupied not the least place, perhaps even the first. Such concerts had occasionally been arranged before, particularly in honor of the drawing-master, who was disliked for his spiteful stupidity. To give a concert meant to accompany the steps of the teacher while he was leaving the classroom with a howling sound made with a closed mouth, so that one could not tell who was actually doing it. Once or twice Burnande got it, but in a mild and considerably muffled form, as he was feared. This time, however, we mustered all our courage. The moment the Frenchman put the school "journal" under his arm, there came, from the extreme flank, a howl which spread in a rolling wave to the desks in front. I, for my part, did what I could. Burnande, who had already stepped through the door, instantly turned back, and stood in the middle of the room, face to face with his enemies, his face pale-green and his eyes darting fire, but without uttering a word. The boys behind the desks, particularly those in the front seats, looked innocence itself. Those in the back seats were busy with their kits as if nothing had happened. After staring at us for half a minute Burnande turned to the door in such a fury that the tails of his coat blew out like sails. The Frenchman was accompanied this time by a unanimous and enthusiastic howl which followed him far down the corridor.

Before the next lesson began there came into the classroom Burnande, Schwannebach, and the class monitor Mayer, who was known among the boys as "Ram" on account of his bulging eyes, strong forehead, and torpid brain. Schwannebach essayed something resembling an introductory speech, all the while circumnavigating with extreme care the hidden reefs of the Russian declensions and conjugations. Burnande breathed revenge. And Mayer scrutinized the boys' faces with his protruding eyes, calling out those known to be sportive, and saying: "You are sure to have been in it." Some boys mildly protested their innocence; others maintained silence. In this way ten or fifteen boys were picked out for detention "without dinner," some for one hour, and some for two hours. The rest were allowed to go home, and I was of their number, although I believe I saw Burnande cast an intensely prying glance at me during the roll-call. I did nothing to obtain exemption. Neither did I accuse myself. I left the school rather with a feeling of regret, as staying with the other boys would have promised a jolly time.

Next morning, when I was on my way to school with the

memory of the previous day's incident barely present in my mind, I was stopped at the gate by one of the punished boys. "Look here," he said, "you're in for trouble. Yesterday Danilov accused you before Mayer, Mayer called Burnande, then the head master came, and they all tried to find out if you were the ringleader."

My heart sank into my boots. And at the same moment the monitor, Peter Pavlovich, emerged. "Go to the head master," he said. The fact that he *had* waited for me at the entrance, and the tone in which he addressed me, augured ill. Inquiring of one doorman after another, I found my way into the mystery-wrapt corridor where the head master's room was, and there I stopped outside his door. The head master passed me, looked at me gravely and shook his head. I stood there, more dead than alive. The head master came out of his room again and only let fall: "All right! All right!" I realized that in point of fact it was not all right at all. A few minutes later teachers began to come out of their room next door, the majority of them hurrying to their classrooms without so much as noticing me. Krizhanovsky answered my bow with a sly grimace which seemed to say: "Got in a mess, my boy. I'm sorry for you, but such is fate." And Burnande, after my courteous bow, came right up to me, bent his spiteful little beard over me, and waving his hands said: "The star student of the second grade is a moral outcast," then turned and walked away. A few minutes later the "Ram" straddled up. "That's the sort of bird you are," he said with apparent satisfaction. "We'll teach you a lesson." Then my long torture commenced. In my classroom, from which I was kept away, there was no lesson: a cross-examination was going on there. Burnande, the head master, Mayer, and the "inspector" Kaminsky formed a supreme investigating committee to inquire into the case of the moral outcast.

It began, as transpired afterward, with one of the punished boys complaining to Mayer during the detention in school: "We have been unjustly punished. The one who made the most noise went scot-free. B. egged the other boys on and shouted himself, and he was allowed to go home. And Carlson, he will tell you so, too."

"I don't believe it," said Mayer, "B. is a well-behaved boy."

But Carlson, the boy who recommended Binneman to me as the cleverest man in Odessa, corroborated the accusation, as did a few others. Mayer called Burnande. Encouraged and urged on by their superiors, infecting one another with their example, there emerged ten or twelve informers from the entire body of boys.

They began to search their memories. A year before B. had said something during a walk about the head master. B. had repeated it to somebody else. B. had taken part in the "concert" to Zmigordsky. Vakker, who was the cause of all the trouble, said in a moving voice: "I cried, as you know, because Gustave Samoilovich gave me the lowest marks, and B. came up to me, put his hand on my shoulder and said: 'Don't cry, Vakker, we will write the inspector-general such a letter that he will dismiss Burnande.' "

"Write to whom?"

"The inspector-general."

"Is that so! And what did you say?"

"I said nothing, of course."

Danilox picked up the story: "That's quite true. B. suggested writing a letter to the inspector-general, but not to sign it, so as not to get expelled, but to let every one write one character in the letter in turn."

"I see," gloated Burnande, "every one a character in turn!"

All of the boys, without exception, were cross-examined. A number of them flatly denied everything—both what did not happen, and what did. One of them was Kostya R., who wept bitterly at seeing his best friend, the star student, so shamefully betrayed. The informers denounced these stubborn deniers as my friends. Panic reigned in the classroom. The majority of the boys closed up and said nothing. For once Danilov was playing first-fiddle, which had never happened to him before, and never did again. I stood in the corridor near the head master's room, next to a yellow polished cupboard, like a man who had committed a grave crime against the state. There the principal witnesses were brought in turn to confront the accused. In the end I was told to go home.

"Go and tell your parents to come here."

"My parents are way down in the country."

"Then tell your guardians."

Only the day before, I had held the undisputed rank of star student, quite a distance ahead of the next boy. Even Mayer had never so much as suspected me. To-day I lay prostrate on the ground, and Danilov, who was known for his laziness and naughtiness, was reviling me in front of the entire class and the authorities of the school. What had happened? Had I come too rashly to the aid of an injured boy who was not my friend and for whom otherwise I had no feeling of sympathy? Or had I placed too much confidence in the united support of the class? I was in no mood for these generalizations, however, while I was returning to the Pokrovsky Alley. With a distorted face and beating heart, in a flood of words and tears, I related what happened. My guardians tried to console me as best they could, though they themselves were greatly perturbed. Fanny Solomonovna went to see the head master, the inspector Krizhanovsky, and Yurchenko, trying to explain, to persuade, and quoting her own experience as a teacher. All this was being done without my knowledge. I sat in my room, with my kit unopened on the table, and moped. Days passed. How would it end? The head master said: "A meeting of the teachers' council will be called to consider the question in its entirety." This sounded awe-inspiring.

The meeting took place. Moissey Filippovich went to hear the decision. I waited for his return with greater excitement than I did in later years for the sentence of the Czar's court.

The entry downstairs resounded with the familiar bang, familiar footsteps mounted the iron staircase, the dining-room door opened, and simultaneously from another room appeared Fanny Solomonovna. Gently I lifted my curtain. "Expelled," said Moissey Filippovich in a voice that betrayed fatigue. "Expelled?" asked Fanny Solomonovna, catching her breath. "Expelled," repeated Moissey Filippovich in a still lower tone. I said nothing, only glanced at Moissey Filippovich and Fanny Solomonovna, and withdrew behind my curtain. During the summer vacation, on a visit to Yanovka, Fanny Solomonovna described the scene: "When this word was uttered he turned all green, so that I became very alarmed about him." I did not cry. I merely pined.

At the teachers' council, three degrees of expulsion were debated: without the right of joining any school; without the right of re-entering the St. Paul *realschule;* and finally, *with* the right of re-entering the latter. The last and most lenient form was selected. I shuddered at the thought of the effect that breaking the news would have on my parents. My guardians did everything in their power to soften the blow. Fanny Solomonovna wrote a long letter to my elder sister, with instructions as to how the news should be broken. I stayed on in Odessa until the end of the school year, and went home for the vacation as usual. During the long evenings, when my father and mother were already asleep, I would relate to my sister and oldest brother how it all happened, impersonating the teachers and the boys. The memory of their own school life was still fresh with my sister and brother. At the same time they regarded themselves as my superiors. Now they shook their heads, and then they burst out laughing over my story. From laughter my sister went on to tears and cried copiously, with her head resting on the table. It was decided then that I was to go on a visit somewhere for a week or two, and while I was away my sister would tell Father everything. She herself was rather frightened by her commission. After the academic failure of my oldest brother, my father's ambition had centred in me. The first years seemed to bear out his hopes, and then suddenly all had gone down with a crash.

Returning to my home from the visit with a boy friend— Grisha, the grandson of Moissey Kharitonovich, the right-handed musician—I instantly perceived that everything was known. Mother welcomed Grisha very cordially, but pretended that she did not see me at all. On the contrary, Father behaved as if nothing had happened. But a few days later, while he was resting in the cool hall after coming home from the fields, he suddenly asked me in the presence of Mother: "Show me how you whistled at your head master. Like this? With two fingers in the mouth?" And illustrating, he burst out laughing. Mother, greatly surprised, kept moving her eyes from Father to myself. On her face a smile struggled with indignation; how could one talk with such levity about such dreadful things? But Father persisted in his demand: "Show how you whistled." And his laughter grew still merrier. Pained as he was, he obviously relished the idea that his offspring, despite his title of the star student, had daring enough to whistle at high officials. In vain did I try to convince him that there was no whistling, but only a peaceful and perfectly innocent howl. He insisted that it was whistling. It ended up with Mother bursting into tears.

I made hardly any effort to prepare for the examinations. What had taken place made me lose, for the time being, all interest in study. I spent a restless summer with ever-recurring flare-ups of ill temper, and about a fortnight before the examinations returned to Odessa, but even there worked very badly. Perhaps the greatest effort I made was in the study of French. At the actual examination, however, Burnande confined himself to a few cursory questions. Other teachers asked even less. I was admitted to the third grade. There I met most of the boys who had either betrayed me, or defended me, or had remained neutral. This determined my personal relations for a long time. Some boys I cut completely; with others who had supported me during these trying moments, I became even more friendly.

Such, one might say, was the first political test I underwent. These were the groups that resulted from that episode: the tale-bearers and the envious at one pole, the frank, courageous boys at the other, and the neutral, vacillating mass in the middle. These three groups never quite disappeared even during the years that followed. I met them again and again in my life, in the most varied circumstances.

The snow was not yet all cleared from the streets—but it was already warm. The housetops, the trees, and the sparrows proclaimed the spring. The fourth-grade boy was walking home, carrying in his hand, against all regulations, a strap from his kit, the reason being that the hook was torn off. The long coat seemed useless and heavy, merely causing one's body to perspire. Fatigue went with it. The boy saw everything in a new light, himself above all. The spring sun stimulated the feeling that there was something immeasurably mightier than the school, the inspector, and the kit hanging aslant on the back—mightier than studying, chess, dinners and even reading and the theatre; in short, than all of one's every-day life. And the longing after this something unfathomed, commanding obedience and rising high above the individual, seized upon the boy's entire being down to the marrow of his bones and called forth the sweet pain of exhaustion.

He came home with a buzzing head, with painful music in his temples. Dropping the kit on the table, he lay down on the bed and, hardly realizing what he was doing, began to weep into the pillow. To find an excuse for his tears, he recalled pitiful scenes from books and from his own life, as if to feed the furnace with fresh fuel, and wept and wept with tears of spring longing. He was in the fourteenth year of his life.

From his childhood the boy had suffered from a disease which the doctors in their official certificates described as chronic catarrh of the digestive tract, and which was closely intertwined with his entire life. Often he had to take medicine, and go on a diet. Nervous shocks nearly always affected his digestion. In the fourth grade, the disease became so acute that it crippled his studies. After a long but unsuccessful course of treatment, the doctors passed sentence: the invalid must be sent to the country.

I received the doctors' verdict with pleasure rather than with regret. But it was necessary to gain the consent of my parents. It was necessary to get a tutor to stay with me in the country to avoid losing a year at school. This meant extra expense, and they did not like extra expense at Yanovka. With the help of Moissey Filippovich, however, the matter was finally arranged. The student G. was engaged as a tutor—a little man with a huge mane of hair, grown noticeably gray on the sides. He was slightly vain, and slightly fantastic, very talkative and utterly lacking in character—one of that type of former undergraduate with an uncompleted education which never succeeds in life. He wrote verse and even had two poems published in the local paper. The two issues were always with him, and he was only too pleased to show them. His relations with me were subject to spasmodic outbursts tending constantly to get worse. At first G. established with me a relationship of ever-growing familiarity, insisting on every occasion that he wanted to be my friend. To this end he showed me the photograph of a certain Claudia and described their rather complicated relations. Then he would suddenly draw back and demand from me the respectful attitude due the teacher from his pupil. This grotesque situation ended badly; there was a violent quarrel, and a final break between us. But even the episode with the tutor was not without effect, whatever one may think of it. Here was a man with graying hair confiding to me the secrets of his association with a woman who in her photograph looked very imposing. This made me feel older.

In the upper grades the teaching of literature passed from Krizhanovsky to the hands of Gamov. The latter was still a young man, fair-haired, rather plump, very short-sighted, and without the least spark of interest in his subject. We dismally tottered along after him from chapter to chapter. To top this off, Gamov was also not punctual and would put off indefinitely the reviewing of our papers. In the fifth grade we were supposed to do four home papers on literature. I began to regard the task with an ever-growing attachment. I read not only the sources indicated by the teacher, but a number of other books as well, copying out facts and passages, altering and appropriating the sentences that caught my imagination, and in general working with a great enthusiasm which did not always stop at the threshold of innocent plagiarism. There were a few other boys who did not regard composition merely as an odious task.

Excitedly—some with fear, others with hope—the fifth-grade boys waited for the grading of their work. But the marks never arrived. The same thing happened in the second quarter of the school year. In the third quarter I handed in a paper which filled an entire pad. A week passed, then a second, and a third—but there was no trace of our work. Cautiously we brought the fact to Gamov's attention. His answer was evasive. At the next lesson Yablonovsky, also an eager composition-writer, put the question pointblank to Gamov: what was the reason for our never learning the fate of our papers, and what did actually happen to them? Gamov sharply told him to shut up. But Yablonovsky would not give up. Knitting his eyebrows still closer together, he began nervously to pull at the top of his desk, and, raising his voice, kept repeating that it was "impossible to go on working like this."

"I must ask you again to keep silent and sit down," answered Gamov. But Yablonovsky would neither sit down nor stop talking. "Please leave the room," shouted Gamov. My relations with Yablonovsky had not been friendly for some time. The affair with Burnande in the second grade taught me to be more circumspect. But here I felt that I could not keep silent. "Anton Mikailovich," I cried, "Yablonovsky is right and we all support him."

"He's right, he's right," echoed other boys. Gamov at first seemed somewhat taken aback, but immediately recovered, and flying into a rage shouted at the top of his voice: "I know myself what to do and when to do it. . . . I don't take orders from you. You are violating the rules. . . ." We had evidently touched some sore spot.

"We only want to see our papers, that's all," a third one chimed in. Gamov was fuming. "Yablonovsky, leave the room at once!" he shouted. Yablonovsky did not budge. "Go out, do go out," came whispers from all sides. Shrugging his shoulders, rolling the whites of his eyes, and stamping heavily with his boots, Yablonovsky left the room, banging the door with all the force he could muster. At the beginning of recess Kaminsky slid into the room on his noiseless rubber soles. This was a bad omen. The room became very quiet. In a husky falsetto voice like a drunkard's, he administered a short, but very stern reproof containing a threat of expulsion from the school, and announced the punishment: Yablonovsky to be put in solitary confinement for twenty-four hours, and to be given a "three" in conduct; for me, twenty-four hours in solitary confinement; and for the third protestant, twelve hours. That was the second hole on my academic road. The case brought no other important consequences. Gamov did not return our papers, in spite of everything. And we too tried to forget the matter.

That year was marked by the death of the Czar. The event seemed tremendous, even incredible, but very distant, like an earthquake in another country. Neither I nor the people about me were at all moved by the Czar's illness, felt any sympathy for him, or any sorrow on account of his death. When I came to school the following morning, the place seemed gripped by something like a great, but causeless panic. "The Czar is dead," said the boys one to another, and did not know what to say next, or how to express their feelings, for they did not realize themselves what this feeling was. But they knew well that there would be no classes, and, without showing it, were pleased at the prospect, particularly those who had not done their home work, or who were afraid of being called down. The janitor directed all comers into the big hall where requiem services were being arranged. The priest in gold spectacles said a few appropriate words: children are grieved when their father dies—how much greater must be the grief when the father of the whole people dies! But there was no grief. The requiem dragged on. It was trying and dull. Everybody was ordered to put a mourning-band around his left arm and to cover the badge on his cap with black muslin. Everything else went on as before.

In the fifth grade, the boys were already exchanging views about going to college and choosing their vocations. A great deal of talk centred on the competitive entrance examinations, on the sternness of the St. Petersburg professors toward the applicants, the tricky problems that were asked, and the specialists in St. Petersburg who coached boys for their examinations. Among the older boys we knew, there were some who went to St. Petersburg year after year, flunked the examinations, prepared again, and again went through the same experience. At the thought of these future trials many a boy felt his heart freeze two years before the time.

The sixth grade passed without incident. Everybody was anxious to escape from the school drudgery as soon as possible. The matriculation examinations were staged with all pomp in the great hall, and with the participation of university professors sent especially by the educational authorities. The head master would open with great solemnity the package received from the inspector-general, which contained the subject for the papers. Its announcement was usually followed by a general sigh of fear, as if everybody had been dipped into icy water. The nervous suspense made one think that the task was utterly beyond one's powers. But further consideration soon revealed that the fears were much exaggerated. As the time drew toward the end of the two hours allotted for each paper, the teachers themselves would help us deceive the vigilance of the regional authorities. Having finished my paper, I did not hand it in immediately but remained in the hall, by a tacit agreement with the inspector Krizhanovsky, and engaged in animated correspondence with those who found themselves in difficulties.

The seventh grade was considered a supplementary one. There was no seventh grade in the St. Paul *realschule*—and this necessitated a transfer to another school. In the interim we found ourselves free citizens. For the occasion everybody outfitted himself in civilian attire. The very evening of the day we received our diplomas, a large group of us disported ourselves in the Summer Garden, where gay cabaret actresses sang on the open stage and where schoolboys were strictly forbidden to enter. We all wore neckties and smoked cigarettes, and there were two bottles of beer adorning the table. Deep in our hearts we were afraid of our own daring. No sooner had we opened the first bottle when the school monitor Wilhelm, nicknamed "the goat" because of his bleating voice, sprang up right before our table. Instinctively we made an effort to rise, and felt our hearts jump. But everything came off well. "You are already here?" said Wilhelm with a tinge of regret in his voice, and graciously shook hands with us. The eldest of the boys, K., wearing a ring on his little finger, nonchalantly invited the monitor to have a glass of beer with us. This was carrying it too far. Wilhelm, with a show of dignity, declined and, hurriedly saying "good-by," walked away in search of the boys who ventured to step over the forbidden threshold of the Garden. With redoubled awareness of our own status we attacked the beer.

The seven years I spent in the school, beginning with the preparatory class, had their joys too. But it would seem that these were not as plentiful as sorrows. The color of my memory of the school, taken as a whole, has remained if not quite black, at least decidedly gray. Above all the episodes of school life, whether gay or sad, towered the régime of soulless, official formalism. It would be difficult to name a single teacher of whom I could think with genuine affection. And yet our school was not the worst. It certainly did teach me a few things: elementary knowledge, the habit of methodical work, and outward discipline. All these came in advantageously in my later life. The same school, however, sowed in me, contrary to its direct purpose, the seeds of enmity for the existing order. These seeds, at any rate, did not fall on barren ground.

CHAPTER V

COUNTRY AND TOWN

THE first nine years of my life, without a break, I spent in the country. During the next seven years I returned there every summer, sometimes also at Christmas and Easter. I was closely bound to Yanovka and all its environs until I was nearly eighteen. Throughout the early part of my childhood the influence of the country was paramount. In the next period, however, it had to defend itself against the influence of the town, and was forced to retreat all along the line.

The country made me familiar with agriculture, the flour-mill, and the American sheaf-binding machine. It brought me into close contact with peasants, the ones who lived near by and came to the flour-mill, and those far-away ones from the Ukrainian districts, who came with a scythe and a bag behind their backs. Much of my country life vanished from my memory or was shoved into the subconscious, but at every new turn some small part of it would emerge, often to help me greatly. The country brought me face to face with the various types of decadence in the gentry, and the types of capitalist aggrandizement. It revealed to me the natural coarseness of many aspects of human relationships, and intensified my feeling for that other urban type of culture, at once more advanced and more contradictory.

It was on my very first vacation that the contrast between town and country impressed itself on my mind. On my journey home I was all impatience. My heart was beating with joy. I longed to see everything again, and to be seen. At Novy-Bug I was met by my father. I showed him my school report, proudly displaying my high marks, and explained that now I was in the first grade and therefore I had to have a full-dress uniform. We were driving by night, in a covered wagon, with a young mill assistant in the place of the coachman. On the steppe, particularly in the dells, one felt a slight draft of cold, misty air, which made my father wrap me in a huge Cossack cloak. I was intoxicated with the change of environment, with

the drive, the recollections, the new impressions, and was very
talkative, running on about the school, the public baths, my
friend Kostya R., the theatre, and so on. I gave full descriptions first of the "Nazar Stodolya," and then of "The Tenant
with a Trombone." My father, sometimes awake, sometimes
asleep, listened to me, and laughed quite a bit. The young assistant shook his head from time to time, and turning to my
father said: "What a story!"

Toward morning I fell asleep, and woke up at Yanovka.
Our house looked terribly small to me now; the home-made
wheat bread seemed gray, and the whole routine of country life
seemed at once familiar and strange. I described the theatre
to my mother and sisters, but not nearly so fervently as I had
to my father. In the workshop I found Victor and David so
changed I could scarcely recognize them—they had grown big-
ger and stronger. But they thought me different, too. From
the first they began to address me with the more respectful
"vy" (you), at which I protested. "Well, what else can I call
you?" retorted David. "You are now a learned man." During my absence Ivan Vasilyevich had married. The servants'
kitchen had been rebuilt and served him as a house, while a
new hut behind the machine-shop had been made over into a
kitchen.

These were not the most important things, however. Something new had grown up like a wall between myself and the
things bound up with my childhood. Everything seemed the
same and yet quite different. Objects and people looked like
counterfeits of themselves. Of course, certain things had
changed during the year. But others seemed changed largely
because I saw them with different eyes. After my first return
home, I began to grow away from my family. At first the
breach revealed itself in trivialities, but as the years went on
it became more and more serious and far-reaching.

The conflicting influences of town and country colored the
entire period of my school life. In the town my relations with
other people were, I felt, more constant. With the exception
of a few conflicts, however violent, such as those with the
teachers of French and Russian, I got along peacefully under
the school and family discipline. This should be attributed
not only to the mode of life in the Schpentzer household, in

which sensible strictness and comparatively high standards in personal relations were the rule, but also to the whole system of life in the city. To be sure, its contradictions were no less marked than those of country life—in fact they were greater—but in town they were more disguised, controlled, and regulated. People of different classes in town came into contact with one another only in their business relations; outside of these they did not exist for one another. In the country everybody lived in open view of everybody else. The relationship between a master and a servant stood out there like a spring in an old couch. My own behavior in the country was more unbalanced and quarrelsome. There were several occasions when I quarrelled even with Fanny Solomonovna, who, on her visits to Yanovka, sometimes cautiously sided with my mother or sisters; and yet in town my relations with her were not only friendly but even affectionate. These clashes sometimes sprang up out of mere trifles. On other occasions, however, something much more important was at their source.

In a freshly laundered duck suit, with a leather belt that had a brass buckle, and a white cap with a glittering yellow badge, I felt that I was simply magnificent. And I had to show everybody. Together with my father, I drove into the field on a day when the harvesting of winter wheat was at its peak. The head mower Arkhip, looking at once sullen and kindly, was leading the way over the hill, followed by eleven mowers and twelve women binders. Twelve scythes were cutting the wheat and the sultry air as well. Arkhip's feet were wrapped in pieces of cloth tightened by a button. The women binders wore torn skirts, or simply shirts of unbleached cotton. From a distance the sound of the mowing-scythes was as if the hot air itself were ringing.

"Well, well, let's see what this winter wheat is like," said Father, taking Arkhip's scythe and stepping into his place. I watched him excitedly. Father made simple, homely movements, as if he were not actually working but only getting ready to begin, and his steps were light and tentative as if he were looking for a place to get a better swing. His scythe was also moving simply, without any swagger about it, and even—or so it seemed—not quite firmly. And yet it was cutting very low and very evenly, with each swift shave laying the ears in a straight belt running along on his left. Arkhip looked on with one eye, clearly approving Father's skill. The attitude of the others varied. Some seemed to be sympathetic, as if they thought the old fellow were no mere novice, while others were indifferent, as if feeling that it was no great achievement to mow what was one's own, and in order to show off, at that. Probably I did not translate their thoughts into exact words, but I had an intense realization of the complicated mechanics of their relations.

After Father had left for another field, I also made an attempt to wield the scythe. "Strike the hay on your heel, boy, on your heel; keep your toes free, don't press." But in my excitement I couldn't quite see where that heel of mine actually was, and on the third swing of the scythe my toes dug right into the earth. "That will soon finish the scythe, if you go on like this," said Arkhip. "You'd better learn from your father." A woman binder, dark-faced and covered with dust, gave me a sneering look. I stepped out of the ranks with decided haste, still in my badge-adorned cap, from under which sweat was coming down in streams. "Go and eat cakes with your mother," came mockingly from behind. It was Mutuzka. I knew that mower, with a skin as dark as his boots. This was his third year at Yanovka. He lived in the village, had his wits about him, was sharp with his tongue, and on occasion in the preceding year, in my hearing and for my special benefit, had spoken nasty but very apt words about his masters. His smartness and daring appealed to my imagination, but his unbridled and shameless scoffing made me boil with impotent hatred. I should have liked to say something to him that would win him over to my side, or, on the contrary, to pull him up with a sharp word of command, but I did not know what to say.

As I returned home from the field I saw a barefooted woman at our door-step. She was sitting on the ground, leaning against the wall, having apparently not courage enough to sit on the stone step. She was the mother of a half-witted shepherd boy, Ignatka, and she had walked seven versts to our house to get one rouble that was owed her. But there was no one in the house, and she could not get her rouble; so she had to wait until evening. It made my heart tighten to look at that figure—the embodiment of poverty and submission.

It was no better next year; in fact, it was worse. I was returning home after a game of croquet when I met my father in the courtyard. He had just arrived from the fields, all covered with dust, worn out and in a bad humor. A peasant, a piebald little man, was stumping behind him on bare, black-heeled feet. "For the Lord's sake, please let me have my cow," he kept saying, swearing that he would do everything to keep it away from the fields. Father answered: "Your cow may eat only ten kopecks' worth of grain, but it will do ten roubles' worth of damage." The peasant kept on beseeching, and in his pleas one could feel his hatred. The scene stirred me to my very marrow. The genial mood I had carried away from the croquet court with its fringe of pear-trees, where I had routed my sisters with flying colors, instantly gave way to a feeling of intense despair. I slipped past my father into my bedroom, and falling flat on the bed, gave myself up to tears, despite my status of a boy of the second grade. Father walked through the hall into the dining-room, with the little peasant pattering behind him up to the door-step. I could hear their voices. Then the peasant left. Mother came from the mill—I could recognize her voice at once; the sound of plates being prepared for dinner came through, and I heard Mother calling me. . . . But I did not answer, and went on weeping. Tears were beginning to yield a sense of blissful pleasure. Then the door opened, and Mother bent over me.

"What's the matter, Lyovochka?"

I made no answer. Mother and Father whispered something to one another.

"Are you upset about that peasant? But we gave him back his cow, and we did not fine him."

"I am not upset about that at all," I answered from under the pillow, painfully ashamed of the cause of my tears.

"And we didn't fine him," Mother said again, with emphasis.

It was Father who had guessed the cause of my sorrow and told Mother. Father noticed much in passing, with one quick glance.

One day when Father was away, a police sergeant, a rude, greedy, and arrogant creature, came down and demanded the workers' passports. He found two overdue. Immediately he called their owners from the field and declared them under arrest, for conveyance to their homes as prisoners. One of them was an old man whose brown neck was shrivelled into deep folds; the other was his young nephew. They dropped to their parched knees on the earthen floor of the hall, first the old man, then the younger one, and bowed their heads to the ground. They kept saying: "Do be merciful—don't ruin us, sir!" The fat and sweating sergeant played with his sword, drank cold milk that had been brought to him from the cellar, and answered: "I give mercy only on feast-days, and this is a weekday." I felt as if I were sitting on fire, and in a broken voice let fall some words of protest. "You'd better mind your own business, young man," the sergeant remarked with stern deliberation, while my elder sister waved her finger at me warningly. The sergeant left with the two laborers.

During my vacation I attended to the bookkeeping, that is, I took turn about with my elder brother and sister, entering in the books the names of laborers employed, the terms of employment, and payments made, whether in kind or in cash. I often assisted my father when wages were paid out, and on those occasions there were sudden, brief flashes of temper between us, which remained suppressed only because of the presence of the laborers. There was never any cheating in the making up of the accounts, but the terms of employment were always interpreted harshly. The laborers, particularly the older ones, sensed that the boy was on their side, and this annoyed Father.

After our clashes, I would go out with a book and would stay away even through dinner. On one such occasion, I was caught in a storm in the fields. There was a continuous cracking of thunder, the steppe rain was gurgling in rivulets, and lightning kept flashing from all sides as if trying to get at me. I went on pacing up and down, all soaked through, in shoes that yelped like dogs, and in a cap that looked like a waterspout. When I returned home I was greeted with sidelong glances and silence. Sister gave me a change of dry clothes and something to eat.

Returning to town after the vacations, I was usually accompanied by my father. As a rule we did not take a porter but carried our luggage ourselves. Father carried the heavier bags, and by his back and distended arms I could see that he was straining himself. I felt sorry for him and tried to carry as much as I could. But when we happened to have with us a heavy box full of gifts from home for the relatives in Odessa, we hired a porter. Father was stingy with his tips, the porter was dissatisfied, and shook his head angrily. I always felt very pained about this. When I travelled alone and had to resort to porters, I spent my pocket-money in no time, looking anxiously into the porter's eyes, and always afraid to give too little. This was a reaction against the closeness at home, and it has persisted throughout my life.

In the country as well as in the town, I lived in a petty-bourgeois environment where the principal effort was directed toward acquisition. In this respect, I cut myself off both from the country of my early childhood and from the town of my youth. The instinct of acquisition, the petty-bourgeois outlook and habits of life—from these I sailed away with a mighty push, and I did so never to return.

In the spheres of religion and nationality, there was no opposition between the country and the town; on the contrary, they complemented one another in various respects. In my father's family there was no strict observance of religion. At first, appearances were kept up through sheer inertia: on holy days my parents journeyed to the synagogue in the colony; Mother abstained from sewing on Saturdays, at least within the sight of others. But all this ceremonial observance of religion lessened as years went on—as the children grew up and the prosperity of the family increased. Father did not believe in God from his youth, and in later years spoke openly about it in front of Mother and the children. Mother preferred to avoid the subject, but when occasion required would raise her eyes in prayer.

When I was about seven or eight years old, belief in God was still regarded in the family as something officially recognized. On one occasion a visiting guest before whom my parents, as was their wont, were boasting about their son, making me show my sketches and recite poetry, asked me the question:

"What do you know of God?"

"God is a sort of man," I answered without hesitation.

But the guest shook his head: "No, God is not a man."

"What is God?" I asked him in my turn, for besides man I

knew only animals and plants. The guest, my father, and my mother exchanged glances with an embarrassed smile, as always happens among grown-ups when children begin to shake the most firmly established conventions.

"God is spirit," said the guest. Now it was I who looked with a smile of confusion at my seniors, trying to read in their faces whether they were serious or joking. But no, it was not a joke. I bowed my head before their knowledge. Soon I got used to the idea that God was spirit. As became a little savage, I connected God with my own "spirit," calling it "soul," and already knowing that "soul," that is, "breath," ends when death comes.* I did not yet know, however, that this doctrine bore the name of "animism."

On my first vacation at home, when I was getting ready to go to sleep on the sofa in the dining-room, I got into a discussion about God with the student Z., who was a visiting guest at Yanovka and slept on the divan. At that time I was not quite sure whether God did exist or not, and did not worry much about it, though I did not mind finding a definite answer.

"Where does the soul go after death?" I asked Z., bending over the pillow.

"Where does it go when a man is asleep?" came the answer.

"Well, it is then still . . ." I argued, trying to keep awake.

"And where does the soul of the horse go when he drops dead?" Z. persisted in his attack.

This answer satisfied me completely, and I fell into a contented sleep.

In the Schpentzer family, religion was not observed at all, not counting the old aunt, who did not matter. My father, however, wanted me to know the Bible in the original, this being one of the marks of his parental vanity, and therefore I took private lessons in the Bible from a very learned old man in Odessa. My studies lasted only a few months and did little to confirm me in the ancestral faith. A suggestion of a double meaning in the words of my teacher, concerning some text in the Bible which we were studying, prompted me to ask a question which I worded very cautiously and diplomatically: "If we

*In Russian "spirit," "soul," and "breath"—respectively "dukh," "dusha," and "dykhaniyé"—derive from the same root.—*Translator.*

accept, as some do, that God does not exist, how did the world come to be?"

"Hm," muttered the teacher, "but you can turn this question against him as well." In this ingenious way did the old man express himself. I realized that the instructor in religion did not believe in God, and this set my mind completely at rest.

The racial and religious composition of my *realschule* was very heterogeneous. Religion was taught respectively by a Russian orthodox priest, a Protestant parson, a Catholic priest, and a Jewish instructor. The Russian priest, a nephew of the archbishop, with the reputation of being a favorite with ladies, was a young and strikingly good-looking man, resembling the portraits of Christ—only of the drawing-room type; he had gold spectacles and abundant golden hair, and was, in brief, impossibly handsome. Before the lesson in religion was to begin, boys of different persuasions would divide into separate groups, and those not of the orthodox Russian faith would leave the classroom, sometimes under the very nose of the Russian priest. On such occasions he put on a special expression, in which contempt was only slightly softened by true Christian forbearance, as he watched the boys walk out.

"Where are you going?" he would ask some boy.

"We are Catholics," came the answer.

"Oh, Catholics!" he repeated, nodding his head, "I see, I see. . . . And you?"

"We are Jews."

"Oh, Jews, I see, Jews! Just so, just so!"

The Catholic priest came like a black shadow, always appearing right against the wall and disappearing so inconspicuously that throughout all my years there I could never get a look at his shaven face. A good-natured man by the name of Ziegelman instructed the Jewish boys in the Bible and the history of the Jewish people. These lessons, conducted in Russian, were never taken seriously by the boys.

In my mental equipment, nationality never occupied an independent place, as it was felt but little in every-day life. It is true that after the laws of 1881, which restricted the rights of Jews in Russia, my father was unable to buy more land, as he was so anxious to do, but could only lease it under cover. This, however, scarcely affected my own position. As son of a prosperous landowner, I belonged to the privileged class rather than to the oppressed. The language in my family and household was Russian-Ukrainian. True enough, the number of Jewish boys allowed to join the schools was limited to a fixed percentage, on account of which I lost one year. But in the school I was always at the top of the grade and was not personally affected by the restrictions.

In my school there was no open baiting of nationalities. To some extent the variety of national elements, not only among the boys but among the masters as well, acted as an important check on such policies. One could sense, however, the existence of a suppressed chauvinism which now and again broke through to the surface. The teacher of history, Lyubimov, showed marked partisanship when questioning a Polish boy about the Catholic persecution of orthodox Russians in White Russia and Lithuania. Mizkevic, a lanky, dark-skinned boy, turned green and stood with his teeth set, without uttering a word. "Well, why don't you speak?" Lyubimov encouraged him, with an expression of sadistic pleasure. One of the boys burst out: "Mizkevic is a Pole and a Catholic." Feigning surprise, Lyubimov drawled: "Is that so? We don't differentiate between nationalities here."

It hurt me quite as much to see the concealed cad in Lyubimov's attitude toward Poles, as to see the spiteful captiousness of Burnande with Germans, or the Russian priest's nodding of his head at the sight of Jews. This national inequality probably was one of the underlying causes of my dissatisfaction with the existing order, but it was lost among all the other phases of social injustice. It never played a leading part—not even a recognized one—in the lists of my grievances.

The feeling of the supremacy of general over particular, of law over fact, of theory over personal experience, took root in my mind at an early age and gained increasing strength as the years advanced. It was the town that played the major rôle in shaping this feeling, a feeling which later became the basis for a philosophic outlook on life. When I heard boys who were studying physics and natural history repeat the superstitious notions about "unlucky" Monday, or about meeting a priest crossing the road, I was utterly indignant. I felt that my intelligence had been insulted, and I was on the verge of doing any mad thing to make them abandon their shameless super-stitions.

While the Yanovka people were spending many weary hours trying to measure the area of a field which had the shape of a trapezoid, I would apply Euclid and get my answer in a couple of minutes. But my computation did not tally with the one obtained by "practical" methods, and they refused to believe it. I would bring out my geometry text-book and swear in the name of science; I would get all excited and use harsh words —and all to no purpose. People refused to see the light of reason, and this drove me to despair.

I engaged in a frantic argument with our village mechanic, Ivan Vasilyevich, who persisted in his belief that he could build a perpetual-motion machine.

The law of the conservation of energy seemed to him merely a fanciful idea which had nothing to do with his problem. "That is all book, and this is practice," he would say. My mind refused to understand or reconcile itself to the fact that men could reject incontrovertible truths in order to accept errors and absurd fancies.

Later, the feeling of the supremacy of the general over the particular became an integral part of my literary and political work. The dull empiricism, the unashamed, cringing worship of the fact which is so often only imaginary, and falsely interpreted at that, were odious to me. Beyond the facts, I looked for laws. Naturally, this led me more than once into hasty and incorrect generalizations, especially in my younger years when my knowledge, book-acquired, and my experience in life were still inadequate. But in every sphere, barring none, I felt that I could move and act only when I held in my hand the thread of the general. The social-revolutionary radicalism which has become the permanent pivot for my whole inner life grew out of this intellectual enmity toward the striving for petty ends, toward out-and-out pragmatism, and toward all that is ideologically without form and theoretically ungeneralized.

I will try to look back, in retrospect, at myself. The boy no doubt was ambitious, quick-tempered, and probably a hard person to get along with. I do not think that he had a feeling of superiority over his schoolmates when he entered the school.

Of course in the country they showed him off proudly to the guests; but then there was no one else to compare him with, and the town boys who came to Yanovka always had the superior advantage of being "gymnasists"; they were older, as well, so that they could be seen only from below. The school, however, is a place where rivalry is bitter. From the moment that he found hmiself at the top of his grade, and quite a distance beyond the boy next behind him, the little visitor from Yanovka felt that he could do better than the others. The boys who became his friends acknowledged his leadership. This could not fail to have some effect on his character. The masters also approved of him, and some, like Krizhanovsky, even singled him out for special attention. On the whole, however, the masters treated him well but without any special interest. The boys were divided: there were good friends among them, there were also enemies.

The boy was not lacking in self-criticism. In this he was inclined to be a little too captious. He was dissatisfied with his intellectual equipment and with some of his peculiarities of character. With time this became even more aggravated. Fiercely, he would catch himself in the act of telling a lie; or he would taunt himself because he had not read all the books that the others mentioned so casually. It is obvious that this was very close to vanity. The thought that he must become better and more intelligent than the rest and acquire a wide knowledge of books, weighed constantly on his mind. He thought about the purpose of Man, and of his own purpose.

One evening, Moissey Filippovich, passing by, stopped and asked me, with feigned solemnity: "What do you think of life, old man?" He often resorted to this mock rhetorical manner that was both pompous and ironic. But this time, I felt as if I were touched to the quick. Yes, I was indeed thinking of life, only I did not know enough to apply this name to my boyish fears for the future. My mentor must have overheard my thoughts. "I seem to have touched the sore spot," he said, changing his tone. Then he slapped me gently on the shoulder, and went to his room.

Did the Schpentzer family have any political views? Those of Moissey Filippovich were moderately liberal, in a humanitarian way. They were lightly touched by vague socialist sympathies, tinged with Populist and Tolstoyan ideas. Political subjects were never openly discussed, especially in my presence; probably that was because they were afraid that I might say something censurable at school, and get myself in trouble. And when casual reference to what was going on or had taken place within the revolutionary movement was made in the grown-ups' conversation, such as, for example, "This was in the year of the assassination of Czar Alexander II," it had the ring of a past as far removed as if they had said, "This was in the year Columbus discovered America." The people who surrounded me were outside of politics.

During my school years I held no political views, nor for that matter had I any desire to acquire them. At the same time my subconscious strivings were tinged by a spirit of opposition. I had an intense hatred of the existing order, of injustice, of tyranny. Whence did it come? It came from the conditions existing during the reign of Alexander III; the high-handedness of the police; the exploitation practised by landlords; the grafting by officials; the nationalistic restrictions; the cases of injustice at school and in the street; the close contact with children, servants and laborers in the country; the conversations in the workshop; the humane spirit in the Schpentzer family; the reading of Nekrassov's poems and of all kinds of other books, and, in general, the entire social atmosphere of the time. This oppositional mood was revealed to me cuttingly in my contact with two classmates, Rodzevich and Kologrivov.

Vladimir Rodzevich was the son of a colonel, and was for a time the second highest in our grade. He persuaded his parents to allow him to invite me to their house on a Sunday. I was received with a certain dryness, but courteously. The colonel and his wife spoke to me very little and as if they were scrutinizing me. During the three or four hours which I spent with the family I stumbled several times upon something that was strange and disconcerting to me, and even inimical; it happened when the conversation casually touched on the subject of religion and the authorities. There was a tone of conservative piety about that house that I felt like a blow on the chest. Vladimir's parents did not let him visit me in my home, and the link between us was broken. After the first revolution in

Odessa, the name of Rodzevich, a member of the Black-Hundred, probably one of the members of this family, was fairly well known.

The case of Kologrivov was even more poignant. He entered the school in the second grade, after Christmas, and was conspicuous among the boys as a tall and awkward stranger. He was gifted with incredible industry; he learned things by heart, anything and everything, whenever he could. By the end of the first month his mind was completely groggy from incessant memorizing. When he was called on by the geography teacher to recite the map lesson, without even waiting for the question he started right in: "Jesus Christ left his command to the world. . . ." It is necessary only to mention that the following hour was to be a lesson in religion.

In conversation with this Kologrivov, who treated me, as the first in the grade, not without respect, I made some critical remarks about the principal and somebody else. "How can you speak of the principal in this way?" asked Kologrivov, sincerely indignant. "And why not?" I answered, with a surprise that was even more sincere. "But he is our chief. If the chief orders you to walk on your head, it is your duty to do as you are told, and not criticise him." He said it in just that way. I was astonished by this expression of a formula. It did not occur to me then that the boy was obviously repeating what he must have heard in his feudal home. And although I had no views of my own, I felt that it would be as impossible for me to accept certain views as to eat wormy food.

Along with the suppressed hostility to the political order in Russia, I began to create, in my imagination, an idealized picture of the foreign world—of Western Europe and America. From scattered remarks and descriptions, I began to visualize a culture which was high in itself and included everybody without exception. Later this became part and parcel of my conception of ideal democracy. Rationalism implied that if anything was accepted as theory, it was of course carried out in practice. For this reason it seemed incredible that people in Europe could have superstitions, that the church could exercise a great influnece there, that in America the whites could persecute the negroes. This idealized picture of the Western world, imperceptibly absorbed from my environment of liberal smug citizenship, persisted later on when I was already formulating revolutionary views. I should probably have been greatly surprised in those years if I had heard—if it had been possible to hear it—that the German Republic which is crowned with a Social-Democratic government admits monarchists within its borders but refuses the right of asylum to revolutionaries. Fortunately, since that time many things have ceased to surprise me. Life has beaten rationalism out of me and has taught me the workings of dialectics. Even Hermann Mueller can no longer surprise me.

CHAPTER VI

THE BREAK

THE political development of Russia, beginning with the middle of the last century, is measured by decades. The sixties—after the Crimean War—were an epoch of enlightenment, our short-lived eighteenth century. During the following decade the intelligentsia were already endeavoring to draw practical conclusions from the theories of enlightenment. The decade began with the movement of going down to the people with revolutionary propaganda; it ended with terrorism. The seventies passed into history mainly as the years of "The People's Will." The best elements of that generation went up in the blaze of the dynamite warfare. The enemy had held all its positions. Then followed a decade of decline, of disenchantment and pessimism, of religious and moral searchings— the eighties. Under the veil of reaction, however, the forces of capitalism were blindly at work. The nineties brought with them workers' strikes and Marxist ideas. The new tide reached its culmination in the first decade of the new century—in the year 1905.

The eighties passed bearing the mark of the Supreme Procurator of the Most Holy Synod, Pobedonostzev, the classical upholder of autocratic power and universal immutability. The liberals regarded him as the pure type of the bureaucrat who did not know life. But this was not true. Pobedonostzev evaluated the contradictions hidden in the depths of the national life far more soberly and seriously than did the liberals. He understood that once the screws were loosened, the pressure from below would tear off the social roof in its entirety and all that not only Pobedonostzev but the liberals as well regarded as the pillars of culture and ethics would dissolve into dust. In his own way, Pobedonostzev saw more profoundly than the liberals. It was not his fault that the processes of history proved mightier than the Byzantine system which he, the inspirer of Alexander III and Nicholas II, had defended with such force.

93

In the dead eighties, when the liberals thought that every-thing had become lifeless, Pobedonostzev still felt beneath his feet a ground-swell—subterranean rumblings. He was not calm even in the calmest years of the reign of Alexander III. "It has been and still is hard, and it is bitter to confess that it will continue so," he wrote to one of his trusted men. "The burden upon my soul does not vanish, for I see and feel every hour the temper of the time and what has come over the peo-ple. . . . Comparing the present with the distant past we feel that we are living in some strange world *where everything is going backward to primeval chaos*—and we feel ourselves help-less in the midst of all this ferment." Pobedonostzev lived to see the year 1905, when the subterranean forces that had so greatly terrified him broke out, and the first deep cracks ap-peared in the foundation and walls of the entire old structure.

The year 1891, memorable for the crop failure and the fam-ine, marks the official date of the political breaking-point in the country. The new decade centred around the labor ques-tion. And not in Russia alone—in 1901 the German Social-Democratic Party adopted its Erfurt programme. Pope Leo XIII issued his encyclical dealing with the condition of the working man. Wilhelm was obsessed by social ideas which consisted of a mixture of insane ignorance and bureaucratic romanticism. The *rapprochement* between the Czar and France guaranteed the inflow of capital funds into Russia. The ap-pointment of Witte to the post of Minister of Finance ushered in an era of industrial protectionism. The stormy development of capitalism bred that very "temper of the time" which had tormented Pobedonostzev with uneasy forebodings.

The political shift in the direction of action cropped up first of all in the midst of the intelligentsia. More and more fre-quently and decisively did the young Marxists resort to action. At the same time the dormant populist movement began to show signs of awakening. In 1893 the first legally printed Marxist work, written by Struve, made its appearance. I was then in my fourteenth year, and still very remote from these matters.

In 1894 Alexander III died. As was usual on such occa-sions, the liberal hopes sought support from the heir to the throne. He replied with a kick. At the audience granted to the Zemstvo leaders, the young Czar described their aspirations for a constitution as "nonsensical dreams." This speech was published in the press. The word-of-mouth report was that the paper from which the Czar had read his speech said "groundless dreams," but in his agitation the Czar had expressed himself more harshly than he intended. I was fifteen at the time. I was unreservedly on the side of the nonsensical dreams, and not on that of the Czar. Vaguely I believed in a gradual development which would bring backward Russia nearer to advanced Europe. Beyond that my political ideas did not go.

Commercial, multi-racial, loudly colored and noisy Odessa remained, to an extraordinary degree, far behind other centres in a political sense. In St. Petersburg, in Moscow, in Kiev, there were already in existence at that time numerous socialist circles in the educational institutions. Odessa had none. In 1895 Friedrich Engels died. Secret reports were read at meetings held in his memory by student groups in the various cities of Russia. I was then in my sixteenth year. But I did not know even the name of Engels, and could hardly say anything definite about Marx. As a matter of fact, I probably had never heard of him.

My political frame of mind while at school was vaguely oppositionist, but no more than that. In my day, revolutionary questions were still unknown among the students. It was whispered that certain groups met at the private gymnasium maintained by the Czech, Novak; that there had been arrests; that Novak, who was our instructor in athletics, had been dismissed and replaced by an army officer. In the environment surrounding the home of the Schpentzers there was dissatisfaction, but the régime was held to be unshakable. The boldest dreamed of a constitution as possible only after several decades. As for Yanovka, the subject was unmentionable there. When I returned to the village after my graduation from school, bringing with me dim democratic ideas, Father, immediately alert, remarked with hostility: "This will not come to pass even in three hundred years." He was convinced of the futility of all reformists' efforts and was apprehensive for his son. In 1921, when he came to me in the Kremlin, after having escaped the Red and White perils with his life, I jestingly asked: "Do you remember what you used to say—that the Czarist order was good for another three hundred years?" The old man smiled slyly and replied in Ukrainian: "This time, let your truth prevail."

In the early nineties, the Tolstoyan tendencies began to die down among the intelligentsia. Marxism was victoriously marching upon the populist movement. Publications of all kinds were filled with the echoes of this ideological struggle. Everywhere there were references to the self-confident young people who called themselves materialists. I encountered all this for the first time in 1896.

The question of personal morals, so intimately connected with the passive ideology of the eighties, touched me in a period when "self-perfection" was to me not so much a matter of theory as an organic demand of my spiritual growth. The problem of "self-perfection," however, quickly became bound up with the question of my outlook on the world in general, which led, in turn, to the fundamental dilemma: populism or Marxism? The conflict of these trends engrossed me, but several years later than the general break in the intellectual concepts of the country. By the time I was approaching the alphabet of economic sciences, and was raising the question in my mind as to whether Russia must go through the stage of capitalism, the Marxists of the older generation had already succeeded in finding a path to the working man and in becoming Social Democrats.

I faced the first crossroads on my path, poorly equipped politically even for a seventeen-year-old boy of that period. Too many questions confronted me all at once, without the necessary sequence and order. Restlessly I cast about me. One thing is certain: even then life had stored within my consciousness a considerable load of social protest. What did it consist of? Sympathy for the down-trodden and indignation over injustice —the latter was perhaps the stronger feeling. Beginning with my earliest childhood, in all the impressions of my daily life human inequality stood out in exceptionally coarse and stark forms. Injustice often assumed the character of impudent license; human dignity was under heel at every step. It is enough for me to recall the flogging of peasants. Even before I had any theories, all these things imprinted themselves deeply on me and piled up a store of impressions of great explosive force. It was perhaps because of this that I seemed to hesitate for a while before reaching the great conclusions which I was impelled to draw from the observations of the first period of my life.

There was also another side to my development. When one generation succeeds another, the dead cling to the living. This was the case with the generation of Russian revolutionists whose early youth developed under the weight of the atmosphere of the eighties. In spite of the large perspectives held out by the new doctrines, the Marxists in reality remained imprisoned by the conservative mood of the eighties, displaying an inability to take bold initiatives, remaining inactive when confronted by obstacles, shoving the revolution into the indefinite future, and inclining generally to regard socialism as a task for centuries of evolution.

In such a home as the Schpentzers', political criticism would have been voiced far more loudly several years before my time or several years later. To my lot fell the most stagnant years. One heard almost no conversation on political topics. Big questions were evaded. It was the same at school. Undoubtedly I imbibed a great deal of the atmosphere of the '80's. And even afterward, when my revolutionary ideas were already taking shape, I would catch myself in an attitude of mistrust of action by the masses, taking a bookish, abstract and therefore sceptical view of the revolution. I had to combat all this within myself, by my thinking, my reading, but mainly by means of experience, until the elements of psychic inertia had been conquered within me.

There is no evil without good. Perhaps the fact that I had consciously to overcome within me the reverberations of the eighties enabled me to approach fundamental problems of mass action in a more serious, concrete and profound manner. Only that is lasting which is gained through combat. All this, however, is related to chapters of my story which are still far ahead.

I attended the seventh grade not in Odessa but in Nikolayev. It was a provincial town and the level of the school was lower there. But my year at Nikolayev—1896—was the turning-point of my youth, for it raised within me the question of my place in human society. I lived in a home where the children were more grown up, and already somewhat in the grip of the newer movements. It is remarkable that at first in conversations I was the stubbornest opponent of "socialist utopias." I played the part of the sceptic who had passed beyond all that. My reaction to political questions was always one of ironic superiority. The landlady in whose home I lodged regarded me with amazement and even cited me as a model—although not always quite confidently—to her own children, who were a little older than I and whose tendencies were toward the Left. But it was merely an unequal struggle on my part for independent judgment. I endeavored to escape the personal influence of such young socialists as I would encounter. This losing battle lasted altogether a few months. The ideas filling the air proved stronger than I, especially since in the depths of my soul I wished for nothing better than to yield to them. My conduct underwent a radical change after several months in Nikolayev. I repudiated my assumption of conservatism and swung Leftward with such speed that it even frightened away some of my new friends. "How did it happen?" my landlady would remark. "And it was all for nothing that I held you up to my children as a model!"

I neglected my studies. The store of knowledge which I had brought from Odessa enabled me, however, to retain somehow my official lead as a star student. More and more frequently I played truant. Once the inspector called on me at home to ascertain the cause of my non-attendance. I felt humiliated beyond words. But the inspector was courteous. He satisfied himself that the home in which I lived and my own room were orderly, and left peaceably. Under my mattress were several illegal political pamphlets.

In Nikolayev I met, in addition to the young people who were drawn toward Marxism, several former exiles who were under police surveillance. These were secondary figures of the period of the decline of the populist movement. At that time Social Democrats were not yet returning from exile, they were going into it. The two cross-movements gave rise to whirlpools of theory. For a time I too was drawn into them. There was an odor of putrefaction emanating from populism. Marxism repelled by its so-called "narrowness." Burning with impatience I tried to grasp the ideas instinctively, but they were not so easy to master. I found no one about me to offer sure guidance. Every new conversation, moreover, forced me to come to the bitter, painful and desperate conclusion that I was ignorant.

I became intimately acquainted with the gardener, Shvigovsky, who was a Czech by origin. He was the first workingman I had known who subscribed to newspapers, read German, knew the classics, and participated freely in the arguments between the Marxists and the populists. His one-room cabin in the garden was the meeting-place for visiting students, former exiles and the local youths. One could obtain a forbidden book through Shvigovsky. The conversations of the exiles were punctuated with the names of the populists, Zhelyabov, Perovskaya, Figner, who were treated not as legendary heroes but as real people with whom the older friends of these exiles—if not they themselves—were familiar. I had a feeling that I was joining a great chain as a tiny link.

I swallowed books, fearful that my entire life would not be long enough to prepare me for action. My reading was nervous, impatient and unsystematic. After wading through the illegal pamphlets of the preceding period, I passed on to "Logic" of John Stuart Mill, then took up Lippert's "Primitive Culture" without completing "Logic." The utilitarianism of Bentham seemed to me the last word in human thought. For several months I was a stanch Benthamist. In the same manner I was carried away by the realistic æsthetics of Chernyshevsky. Without having finished Lippert, I threw myself upon the history of the French Revolution by Mignet. Each book lived separately for me, with no place in a unified system. My striving for a system became tense, sometimes savage. At the same time, I would be repelled by Marxism partly because it seemed a completed system.

I began to read newspapers, not as I had read them in Odessa, but with a political mind. The most authoritative daily at the time was the liberal *Russkiya Vedomosti* of Moscow. We studied rather than read it, beginning with the impotent, professorial editorials and ending with the scientific articles. The foreign correspondence, especially from Berlin, was the pride of the newspaper. It was from the *Russkiya*

Vedomosti that I first formed a picture of the political life of
western Europe, especially of the parliamentary parties. It
is difficult to-day to recall the agitation with which we followed
the speeches of Bebel and even those of Eugene Richter. And
to this day I remember the phrase which Dashinsky flung in
the face of the police when they entered the house of parliament: "I represent thirty thousand workers and peasants of
Galicia—who will dare touch me?" We pictured the Gali-
cian revolutionist as a titanic figure. The theatrical stage of
parliamentarism, alas! cruelly deceived us. The successes of
German socialism, the presidential elections in the United
States, the free-for-alls in the Austrian Reichsrat, the intrigues
of the French royalists, all of this absorbed us far more than
the personal fate of any one of us.

Meanwhile my relations with my family were growing worse.
On one of his trips to Nikolayev to market grain, my father
somehow learned of my new acquaintances. He sensed the
approach of danger, but hoped to prevent it by the power of
his parental authority. We had several stormy scenes. I un-
compromisingly defended my independence, my right to follow
my own path. It ended with my refusing to accept material
aid from home. I left my lodgings and went to live with
Shvigovsky, who was now leasing another garden with a more
spacious cottage. Here six of us led a communal life. During the summer one or two tubercular students seeking fresh
air joined us. I began to give private lessons. We led a spartan
existence, without bed-linen, and got along on stews which
we prepared ourselves. We wore blue smocks, round straw hats
and black canes. In town it was rumored that we had joined
a secret organization. We read without method, we argued
without restraint, we peered into the future passionately, and
were happy in our own way.

After a while we organized a society for the distribution of
useful books among the people. We collected dues and bought
cheap editions, but were unable to disseminate them. In
Shvigovsky's garden there worked a hired laborer and an
apprentice. We focussed upon them, first of all, our efforts at
enlightenment. But the laborer turned out to be a disguised
gendarme who had been planted in our midst expressly to
watch us. His name was Kirill Tkhorzhevsky. He had also

put the apprentice in touch with the gendarmerie. The latter stole from us a large package of popular books and took it to headquarters. This beginning was clearly inauspicious, but we firmly hoped for success in the future.

I wrote a polemical article for a populist periodical in Odessa, taking issue with the first Marxist journal. The article had more epigraphs, quotations and venom than it had content. I mailed the article and a week later made a trip to find out its fate. The editor, through large glasses, eyed with sympathy an author whose head displayed an enormous mop of hair but whose face did not show a trace of beard. The article never saw the light. No one was the loser—least of all myself.

When the board of directors of the public library raised the annual fee from five to six roubles, we perceived an attempt to get away from democracy, and sounded an alarm. For several weeks we did nothing but prepare for a general meeting of the library members. We emptied all our democratic pockets, collecting roubles and half-roubles, and with this fund registered more radical members, many of whom not only lacked the six roubles but also were under the twenty-year age limit required by the constitution. We turned the library application-book into a collection of fiery leaflets. When the annual meeting was called, two parties appeared: on the one hand, officials, teachers, liberal landlords, and naval officers; on the other hand, we—the democracy. Victory was ours along the entire front. We restored the five-rouble fee and elected a new board.

Casting about for activities, we decided to organize a university on a basis of mutual instruction. There were about twenty students. My department was sociology. That was high-sounding. I prepared for my course with all my powers, but after two lectures, which came off satisfactorily, I suddenly realized that my resources had been exhausted. The second lecturer, whose course was the French Revolution, became confused as soon as he began and promised to deliver his lecture in writing. Of course he failed to fulfil his promise, and that was the end of the enterprise.

I then decided, with the second lecturer, the elder of the brothers Sokolovsky, to write a play. We even left the commune temporarily for that purpose, and hid ourselves in a room without leaving any address. Our play was full of social tendencies, against a background of the conflict of generations. Although the two dramatists regarded Marxism with only half-trust, nevertheless the populist in the play was a feeble character, while all the courage, youth and hope were with the young Marxists. Such is the power of time. The romantic element found expression in the love tendered by a revolutionist of the older generation, who had been crushed by life, to a young Marxist girl, but she handed it back with a merciless speech about the failure of populism.

The work on the play was no mean task. At times we wrote together, driving and correcting each other; at other times we divided the acts into sections, and each of us would devote his day to the preparation of a scene or a monologue. We had, it must be said, no shortage of monologues. Sokolovsky would return from his work toward evening, and then would proceed freely to revise the whimpering speeches of the hero of the seventies whose life had been crushed. I would return from my private lessons or from Shvigovsky's. The daughter of the landlady would put up a samovar for us. Sokolovsky would pull out from his pockets some bread and sausage. Separated by a mysterious armor from the rest of the world, the dramatists would spend the balance of the evening in intensive labor. We completed the first act, even providing the proper curtain effect. The remaining acts, four in number, were drafted. The farther we got into it, however, the more we cooled. After a while we arrived at the conclusion that we must give up our mysterious room and postpone the completion of the drama to some future date. The roll of manuscripts was taken by Sokolovsky to another lodging. Later, when we found ourselves in the Odessa prison, Sokolovsky made an attempt through his relatives to locate the manuscript. Perhaps the thought occurred to him that exile would be favorable for the completion of our dramatic opus. But the manuscript was no more, having vanished without trace. In all probability the people in whose home it had been left considered it prudent to throw it in the fire upon the arrest of its ill-fated authors. It is not difficult for me to reconcile myself to its fate, especially since, in the course of my subsequent and none too smooth life, I have lost manuscripts of incomparably greater value.

CHAPTER VII

MY FIRST REVOLUTIONARY
ORGANIZATION

IN the autumn of 1896, I visited the country, after all; but the visit resulted only in a brief truce. Father wanted me to become an engineer, whereas I hesitated between pure mathematics, to which I was very strongly attracted, and Revolution, which little by little was taking possession of me. Every time this question arose there was an acute family crisis. Everybody looked depressed, and seemed to suffer intensely; my elder sister would weep furtively, and nobody knew what to do about it. One of my uncles, an engineer and owner of a plant in Odessa, who was staying in the country with us, persuaded me to come and visit him in the city. This was at least a temporary relief from the *impasse*.

I stayed with my uncle for a few weeks. We were constantly discussing profit and surplus value. My uncle was better at acquiring profits than explaining them. And meanwhile I did nothing about registering for the course in mathematics in the University. I stayed on in Odessa, still looking for something. What was I trying to find? Actually, it was myself. I made casual acquaintances among workers, obtained illegal literature, tutored some private pupils, gave surreptitious lectures to the older boys of the Trade School, and engaged in arguments with the Marxists, still trying to hold fast to my old views. With the last autumn steamer, I left for Nikolayev, and resumed my quarters with Shvigovsky in the garden.

And the same old business started in again. We discussed the latest numbers of the radical magazines and argued about Darwinism; we were vaguely preparing, and also waiting. What was it in particular that impelled us to start the revolutionary propaganda? It is difficult to say. The impulse originated within us. In the intellectual circles in which I moved, nobody did any actual revolutionary work. We realized that between our endless tea-table discussions and revolutionary organization there was a vast gulf. We knew that any contacts with workers demanded secret, highly "conspiratory" methods. And we pronounced the word solemnly, with a reverence that was almost mystic. We had no doubt that in the end we would go from the discussions at the tea-table to "conspiratia"; but nobody was definite as to how and when the change would take place. In excusing our delay, we usually told each other that we must prepare; and we weren't so far wrong, after all.

But apparently there had been some change in the air which brought us abruptly onto the road of revolutionary propaganda. The change did not actually take place in Nikolayev alone, but throughout the country, especially in the capitals. In 1896, the famous weavers' strikes broke out in St. Petersburg. This put new life into the intelligentsia. The students gained courage, sensing the awakening of the heavy reserves. In the summer, at Christmas, and at Easter, dozens of students came down to Nikolayev, bringing with them tales of the upheaval in St. Petersburg, Moscow, and Kiev. Some of them had been expelled from universities—boys just out of the *gymnasium* returning with the haloes of heroes. In February, 1897, a woman student, Vetrova, burned herself to death in the Peter-Paul fortress. This tragedy, which has never been fully explained, stirred every one deeply. Disturbances took place in the university cities; arrests and banishments became more frequent.

I started my revolutionary work to the accompaniment of the Vetrova demonstrations. It happened in this way: I was walking along the street with a younger member of our commune, Grigory Sokolovsky, a boy about my age. "It's about time we started," I said.

"Yes, it is about time," he answered.

"But how?"

"That's it, how?"

"We must find workers, not wait for anybody or ask anybody, but just find workers, and set to it."

"I think we can find them," said Sokolovsky. "I used to know a watchman who worked on the boulevard. He belonged to the Bible Sect. I think I'll look him up."

The same day Sokolovsky went to the boulevard to see the Biblist. He was no longer there. But he found there a woman who had a friend who also belonged to some religious sect.

Through this friend of the woman he didn't know, Sokolovsky, on that very day, made the acquaintance of several workers, among them an electrician, Ivan Andreyevitch Mukhin, who soon became the most prominent figure in our organization. Sokolovsky returned from his search all on fire. "Such men! They are the real thing!"

Next day five or six of us were sitting in an inn. The deafening music of the automatic organ screened our conversation from the rest. Mukhin, a thin man with a pointed beard and a sort of shrewd, apprehensive look, watched me through a half-closed left eye, amiably scanning my still beardless face. In detail, with well-calculated pauses, he explained: "The Gospels for me, in this business, are just a peg. I begin with religion, and then switch off to life. The other day I explained the whole truth to the Stundists with navy-beans."

"What do you mean, navy-beans?"

"It's very simple. I put a bean on the table and say, 'This is the Czar.' Around it, I place more beans. 'These are ministers, bishops, generals, and over there the gentry and merchants. And in this other heap, the plain people.' Now, I ask, 'Where is the Czar?' They point to the centre. 'Where are the ministers?' They point to those around. Just as I have told them, they answer. Now, wait," and at this point Mukhin completely closed his left eye and paused. "Then I scramble all the beans together," he went on. "I say, 'Now tell me where is the Czar? the ministers?' And they answer me, 'Who can tell? You can't spot them now.' . . . 'Just what I say. You can't spot them now.' And so I say, 'All beans should be scrambled.' "

I was so thrilled at this story that I was all in a sweat. This was the real thing, whereas we had only been guessing and waiting and subtilizing. The music of the automatic organ was the "conspiratia"; Mukhin's navy-beans, destroying the mechanics of the class system, were the revolutionary propaganda.

"Only how to scramble them, damn them, that's the problem," Mukhin said, in a different tone, and looked sternly at me with both eyes. "That's not navy-beans, is it?" And this time he waited for my answer.

From that day we plunged headlong into the work. We had

no older men to direct us. Our own experience was inadequate. But not once did we run into difficulties or get confused. One thing evolved from another as inevitably as in our conversation with Mukhin at the inn.

At the end of the last century the pivot of the economic development of Russia was shifting swiftly to the southeast. Great plants were being built one after another in the South, two in Nikolayev. In 1897, the number of workers in the Nikolayev plants amounted to 8,000, in addition to which there were 2,000 workers in various trades. The intellectual level of the workers was comparatively high, as were their earnings. The illiterates were few. The place that the revolutionary organizations came to hold later was then filled to some extent by the religious sects which engaged in successful warfare with the official religion. In the absence of political disorders, the secret police in Nikolayev were slumbering peacefully. They played into our hands admirably. If they had been awake, we would have been arrested during the very first weeks of our activity. But we were the pioneers and benefited by it. We shook up the police only after we had shaken up the workers.

When I made the acquaintance of Mukhin and his friends, I called myself by the name of Lvov. It was not easy for me to tell this first "conspiratory" lie; in fact, it was really painful to "deceive" people with whom one intended to be associated for such a great and noble cause. But the nickname of Lvov soon stuck to me, and I got used to it myself.

The workers streamed toward us as if they had been waiting for this. They all brought friends; some came with their wives, and a few older men joined the groups with their sons. We never sought them out; they looked for us. Young and inexperienced leaders that we were, we were soon overwhelmed by the movement we had started. Every word of ours met with a response. As many as twenty and twenty-five or more of the workers gathered at our secret readings and discussions, held in houses, in the woods, or on the river. The predominating element was composed of highly skilled workers who earned fairly good wages. They already had an eight-hour day at the Nikolayev ship-building yards; they were not interested in strikes; what they wanted was justice in social relations. They called themselves Baptists, or Stundists, or Evangelical

Christians, but theirs was not a dogmatic sectarianism. The workers were simply breaking away from orthodoxy, and baptism became a temporary phase for them in their progress toward revolution. During the first weeks of our conversations, some of them still used sectarian expressions, and often made comparisons with the period of the early Christians. But nearly all of them soon dropped this way of speaking when they found that they were only a laughing-stock for the younger men.

Even to this day the more striking figures among them seem alive to me. There was the cabinetmaker in his bowler, Korotkov, who had done with all mystics long ago, a jocular fellow and a rhymester who would say solemnly, "I am a ratiolist," meaning a rationalist. And when Taras Savelyevitch, an old evangelist and a grandfather, would begin, for the hundredth time, to talk about the early Christians, who like ourselves met secretly, Korotkov would cut him short with "A fig for your theology!" and toss his bowler indignantly up into the trees. He would wait for a while and then go into the woods in search of it. This all happened in the forest on the dunes.

Many of the workers were so infected by the new ideas that they began to compose verses. Korotkov wrote the "Proletarian March" which began this way: "We are the alphas and omegas, the beginnings and endings." Nesterenko, a carpenter, who, like his son, was a member of the group of Alexandra Lvovna Sokolovskaya, composed a song about Karl Marx in Ukrainian, and we sang it in chorus. Nesterenko himself, however, ended very badly. He got in with the police and betrayed the whole organization.

A young laborer, Yefimov, a blond giant with blue eyes, who came of an officer's family and was not only literate but really well read, lived in the slums of the town. I found him in an eating-place patronized by tramps. He worked in the harbor as a longshoreman; he neither smoked nor drank. He was reserved and well-mannered. But there must have been something mysterious about his life, despite the fact that he was only twenty-one, to account for his constant gloominess. He soon confided in me that he had been introduced to some members of the secret society of Narodovoltzi,* and offered to put me in touch with them. Three of us, Mukhin, Yefimov and I,

* Members of the Terrorist *Narodnaya Volya* (*The People's Will*).—*Translator.*

were sitting drinking tea in the noisy "Russia" inn, at the same time listening to the deafening music of the organ and waiting. At last, Yefimov indicated to us with his eyes the figure of a big, stout man with a small beard. "There he is."

The man sat at a table by himself and kept on drinking tea. Then he began to put on his coat, and with a mechanical movement of his hand, crossed himself as he looked at the ikons. "What! Is he the 'Narodovoletz'?" Mukhin exclaimed in a hushed voice. The "Narodovoletz" avoided meeting us, giving Yefimov some vague excuse. The incident has always remained a mystery to me. Yefimov himself soon squared his accounts with life by asphyxiating himself with coal-gas. It is quite possible that the blue-eyed giant was a tool for some spy—or conceivably something even worse.

Mukhin, who was an electrician by trade, installed a complicated system of signalling in his apartment for use in case of police raids. He was twenty-seven, but so full of practical wisdom and so rich in experience of life that he seemed almost old to me. A tubercular, he would cough blood. He remained a revolutionary throughout his life. After one exile and a prison term, he was exiled again. I met him again after twenty-three years at the conference of the Ukrainian Communist Party at Kharkoff. We sat raking up the past as we told each other of the fate that had overtaken many of the group with whom we had been associated at the dawn of the revolution. At the conference Mukhin was elected to the central control committee of the Ukrainian Communist Party. He had surely earned the honor. But soon after that he was laid low by illness. He never recovered.

Immediately after we had come to know each other, Mukhin introduced me to a friend of his, another sectarian, Babenko, who had a little house of his own with apple-trees in the courtyard. Babenko was lame; a slow man who was always sober. He taught me to drink tea with apple instead of lemon. He was arrested with others of our group and spent some time in prison before he returned to Nikolayev again. But Fate separated us. It was only in 1925 that I happened to read in some paper that a Babenko, a former member of the South Russian Labor Union, was living in the Province of Kuban. By then, his legs were completely paralyzed. Somehow I managed, at a time when things were already difficult for me, to have the old man transferred to Essentuki to take the cure. He regained the use of his legs. I visited him in the sanitarium. He didn't even know that Trotsky and Lvov were one and the same man. Again we drank tea with apple and talked about the past. I can just imagine his surprise when he heard that Trotsky was a counter-revolutionary.

There were many other interesting figures, too many to enumerate. There was the fine younger generation that had been trained in the technical school of the shipyards, and was very cultured. A mere suggestion from the instructor was enough to enable them to grasp the whole trend of his thought. We found the workers more susceptible to revolutionary propaganda than we had ever in our wildest dreams imagined. The amazing effectiveness of our work fairly intoxicated us. From revolutionary tales, we knew that the workers won over by propaganda were usually to be counted in single numbers. A revolutionary who converted two or three men to socialism thought he had done a good piece of work, whereas, with us, the number of workers who joined or wanted to join the groups seemed practically unlimited. The only shortage was in the matter of instructors and in literature. The teachers had to snatch from each other in turn the single soiled copy of the Communist Manifesto by Marx and Engels that had been transcribed by many hands in Odessa, with many gaps and mutilations of the text.

Soon we began to produce a literature of our own; this was, properly speaking, the beginning of my literary work, which almost coincided with the start of my revolutionary activities. I wrote proclamations and articles, and printed them all out in longhand for the hectograph. At that time we didn't even know of the existence of typewriters. I printed the letters with the utmost care, considering it a point of honor to make them clear enough so that even the less literate could read our proclamations without any trouble. It took me about two hours to a page. Sometimes I didn't even unbend my back for a week, cutting my work short only for meetings and study in the groups. But what a satisfied feeling I had when I received the information from mills and workshops that the workers read voraciously the mysterious sheets printed in purple ink, passing them about from hand to hand as they discussed them! They pictured the author as a strange and mighty person who in some mysterious way had penetrated into the mills and knew what was going on in the workshops, and twenty-four hours later passed his comments on events in newly printed handbills.

At first we made the hectograph and printed the proclamations in our rooms at night. One of us would stand guard in the courtyard. In the open stove we had kerosene and matches ready to burn the tell-tale things in case of danger. Everything was very crude, but the police of Nikolayev were no more experienced than we were. Later on, we transferred the printing-press to the apartment of a middle-aged worker who had lost his sight through an accident in one of the shops. He placed his apartment at our disposal unhesitatingly. He would say with a low laugh, "Everywhere is prison for a blind man." Gradually we got together at his place a large supply of glycerine, gelatine and paper. We worked at night. The slovenly room, with a ceiling that came low over our heads, had a poverty-stricken look about it. We cooked our revolutionary brew on his iron stove, pouring it out on a tin sheet. As he helped us, the blind man moved about the half-dark room with more assurance than we did. Two of the workers, a young boy and girl, would watch reverently as I pulled the freshly printed sheets off the hectograph, and then would exchange glances. If it had been possible for any one to look at all this with a "sober" eye, at this group of young people scurrying about in the half-darkness around a miserable hectograph, what a sorry, fantastic thing it would have seemed to imagine that they could, in this way, overthrow a mighty state that was centuries old! And yet this sorry fantasy became a reality within a single generation; and only eight years separated those nights from 1905, and not quite twenty from 1917.

Word-of-mouth propaganda never gave me the same satisfaction as the printed bills did at that time. My knowledge was inadequate, and I didn't know how to present it effectively. We made no real speeches in the full sense of the word. Only once, in the woods on May-day, did I have to make one, and it embarrassed me greatly. Every word I uttered seemed horribly false. On the other hand, when I talked to the groups it wasn't so bad. As a rule, however, the revolutionary work went on at full speed. I established and developed contacts with Odessa. Evenings I would go to the pier, pay a rouble for a third-class ticket, and lie down on the deck of the steamer near the funnel, with my jacket under my head and my overcoat to cover me; in the morning I would wake up in Odessa and seek out the people I knew there. Then I would return the next night, so as never to waste any time in travelling. My contacts in Odessa suddenly increased in number. At the entrance of the Public Library, I met a spectacled worker. We looked at each other closely and understood. He was Albert Polyak, a compositor, who later organized the famous central printing-press of the party. My acquaintance with him marked an epoch in the life of our organization. Within a few days after I met him, I brought back with me to Nikolayev a travelling-bag full of "illegal" literature from abroad; new propaganda pamphlets in gaily colored covers. We kept opening the bag to look admiringly at our treasure. The pamphlets were circulated in no time, and increased our authority in labor circles.

From Polyak I accidentally learned in conversation that the mechanic Shrentsel, who had been posing as a full-fledged engineer and had been trying to wedge his way into our group, was an informer of long standing. This Shrentsel was a stupid and importunate fellow who always wore a uniform cap with a badge. Instinctively we never trusted him. But he did learn something about a few of us. I invited him to Mukhin's apartment, and told his life-story in detail, omitting his name. He became utterly frantic. We threatened to give him short shrift if he betrayed us. Apparently it had its effect, because he left us alone for three months after that. But when we were arrested, as if to get even with us Shrentsel piled horror on horror in his evidence against us.

We called our organization the South Russian Workers' Union, intending to include workers from other towns. I drafted our constitution along Social Democratic lines. The mill authorities tried to offset our influence through speakers of their own. We would answer them the next day with new proclamations. This duel of words aroused not only the workers but a great many of the citizens as well. The whole town was alive with talk about revolutionaries who were flooding the mills with their handbills. Our names were on every tongue. Still the police delayed. They refused to believe that "those young brats from the garden" were capable of carrying on any such campaign. They suspected that there were more experienced leaders behind us, probably old exiles. This gave us two or three additional months in which to work. Finally our movements were so closely watched that the police couldn't help but discover one group after another. So we decided to leave Nikolayev for a few weeks, to put the police off our track. I was supposed to go to my family in the country; Sokolovskaya, with her brother, to Ekaterinoslav, and so on. At the same time, we firmly resolved not to hide in case of wholesale arrests, but to let ourselves be taken, so that the police could not say to the workers: "Your leaders have deserted you."

Some time before I was supposed to leave, Nesterenko insisted that I should hand over a bundle of proclamations to him in person. He fixed as the meeting-place behind the cemetery, late at night. There was deep snow on the ground; the moon was shining. Beyond the cemetery you could see a wide desertlike expanse. I found him at the appointed spot. Just as I was handing him a packet that I took out from under my coat, some one detached himself from the cemetery wall and walked past us, touching Nesterenko with his elbow.

"Who is that?" I asked, in surprise.

"I don't know," answered Nesterenko as he watched the other man walk off. At that time he was already working with the police, but it never entered my mind to suspect him.

On the twenty-eighth of January, 1898, there were mass arrests. Altogether, over two hundred people were taken. The police applied the scourge. One of those arrested, a soldier named Sokolov, was driven to throw himself from the second floor of the prison; he was merely badly bruised. Another, Levandovsky, went insane. There were still other victims.

Among those arrested, there were many who got there by accident. A few of those on whom we were relying deserted us, and even in some instances betrayed us. On the other hand, some who had been quite inconspicuous in our ranks showed great strength of character. For instance, there was a turner, a German named August Dorn, a man about fifty years old, who for some unknown reason was detained in prison for a long time, although he had only visited our group a few times. He behaved magnificently, and kept singing gay and, one must admit, not always puritanical German songs at the top of his voice. He made jokes in pigeon-Russian, and kept up the spirits of the young. In the Moscow transfer prison where we were detained, all of us in the same cell, Dorn would address the samovar mockingly, ask it to come over, and then retort, "You won't? Well, then Dorn will come to you." Although this was repeated every day, we always good-naturedly laughed at it.

The Nikolayev organization was hard hit, but it did not disappear. Others soon replaced us. Both the revolutionaries and the police were growing in experience.

CHAPTER VIII

MY FIRST PRISONS

D URING the raids of January, 1898, I was arrested, not in Nikolayev but on the estate of a wealthy landowner, Sokovnin, where Shvigovsky had found a job as a gardener. I had stopped off there on the way from Yanovka to Nikolayev with a large brief-case filled with manuscripts, drawings, letters, and all manner of other "illegal" material. Shvigovsky hid the dangerous packages for the night in a hole, along with cabbages; and at sunrise, when he was going out to plant his trees, he took it out again to turn it over to me for our work. It was just at that very moment that the police suddenly invaded the place. Shvigovsky managed to drop the package behind a water-barrel, when he was in the hall, and whispered to the housekeeper, who gave us our dinner under supervision of the police, to take it away from there and hide it. The old woman decided that the best thing was to bury it under the snow in the garden. We were quite sure that the papers would never get into the hands of our enemies. When spring came the snow melted away, but a fresh crop of green grass covered the package, which had swollen somewhat with the spring rains.

We were still in prison. It was summer. A workman was cutting the grass in the garden when two of his boys who were playing there stumbled on the package and gave it to their father. And he, in turn, took it to the landowner, who was so terrified at the sight of it that he went to Nikolayev at once and turned it over to the chief of the secret police. The handwriting on the manuscripts was evidence against many of our people.

The old prison in Nikolayev had no decent accommodation for political prisoners, especially for so many of them. I was put into the same cell with a young bookbinder named Yavitch. The cell was a very large one; it could hold about thirty, but there was no furniture of any sort, and it had very little heat. There was a big square opening in the door that looked out on an open corridor leading straight into the courtyard. The January frosts were very bitter. A straw mattress was spread on the floor for us to sleep on at night, and was taken away at six o'clock in the morning. It was torture to get up and dress ourselves. Yavitch and I would sit on the floor, in hats, overcoats and rubbers, pressing close to one another and leaning against the stove, which was barely warm, and would dream away for two hours or more at a time. It was the happiest part of the day for us. We were not being called up for cross-examination, so we would run back and forth from one corner to the other, trying to keep warm; we talked about the past and hoped wonderingly about our future. I began to teach Yavitch something about the sciences. Three weeks passed in this way.

Then there was a change. With all my belongings, I was summoned to the prison office and given over to two tall gendarmes, who drove me by horse to a prison at Kherson. It was a building even older than the other. My cell was roomy, but it had only a narrow window that did not open, and was protected by heavy iron bars through which little light could enter. My isolation was absolute and hopeless. There was no walking, nor were there any neighbors. I couldn't see anything through my window, which had been entirely sealed up for the winter. I got no parcels from outside, and I had no tea or sugar. Prisoner's stew was given to me once a day, for dinner. A ration of rye bread with salt was breakfast and supper. I had long discussions with myself as to whether I should increase my morning portion at the expense of the evening one. The morning arguments in favor of an increase seemed quite senseless and criminal at night; at supper-time, I hated the person who had treated himself at breakfast. I didn't have a change of linen. For three months I had to wear the same underwear, and I had no soap. The vermin there were eating me alive. I would set myself to taking one thousand, one hundred and eleven steps on the diagonal. That was my nineteenth year. The solitude was unbroken, worse than any I ever experienced afterward, although I served time in nearly twenty prisons. I didn't have even a book, a piece of paper or a pencil. The cell was never aired. The only way I could gauge the comparative purity of the air was by the grimace that twisted the face of the assistant warden when he sometimes visited me.

Biting off a piece of the prison bread, I would compose verses while I walked on the diagonal. I turned the populist song "Dubinushka" into a proletarian "Machinushka," and I composed a revolutionary "Kamarinsky." Although they were most mediocre, these verses became very popular later on. They are reprinted in the song-books even to-day. There were times, however, when I was sick with loneliness. And on such occasions I would be exaggeratedly firm with myself and count out another one thousand, one hundred and eleven steps in shoes already worn out.

At the end of the third month, when a straw-filled bag, prison-bread, and lice were the fixed elements of existence, as much so as day and night, one evening the guards brought me a great bundle of things from that other, utterly fantastic world; there were fresh linen, covers and a pillow, white bread, tea, sugar, ham, canned foods, apples, oranges—yes, big bright-colored oranges! Even to-day, after thirty-one years, I list all these marvellous things with emotion, and I even pull myself up for having forgotten the jar of jam, the soap and the comb for my hair. "Your mother sent them," said the assistant warden. And little as I knew about reading the thoughts of people in those days, I could tell from his tone that he had been bribed.

A little while later, I was taken on a steamer to Odessa, where I was put into solitary confinement in a prison built only a few years before, and the last word in technical equipment. After Nikolayev and Kherson, the Odessa prison seemed a perfect place. Tapping, notes, "telephone," and shouting through windows—in other words, communication service—were continuous. I tapped my verses written at Kherson to my neighbors, and they sent me news in return. By way of the window, Shvigovsky managed to tell me of the discovery of the brief-case, so that I had no trouble in avoiding the trap that Lieutenant-Colonel Dremlyuga set for me. At that time, I must explain, we had not yet begun to refuse to give evidence, as we did a few years later.

The prison was overcrowded after the thoroughgoing spring arrests. On March 1st, 1898, while I was still at Kherson, the first congress of the Social Democratic Party met at Minsk and drew up its constitution. There were nine members there, and most of them were caught in a wave of arrests that followed their meeting. A few months afterward, no one talked about the congress any more. But what followed it affected the history of man. The manifesto adopted there limned the future of political struggle as follows: "The farther we go to the East of Europe, the more cowardly and dishonest, in a political sense, do we find the *bourgeoisie;* and the greater, correspondingly, becomes the political and cultural task confronting the proletariat." There is a certain historical piquancy in the fact that the author of the manifesto was the notorious Peter Struve, who later became the leader of liberalism, and still later the publicist of the clerical and monarchist reaction.

During the first few months of my stay in the prison in Odessa, I received no books from the outside, and so I had to be content with the prison library, which was made up mostly of conservative historical and religious magazines covering several years. I studied them insatiably, and learned through them to know all the sects and heresies of ancient and modern times, all the advantages of the orthodox church service, and the best arguments against Catholicism, Protestantism, Tolstoyism, and Darwinism. "The Christian consciousness," I read in the *Orthodox Review,* "loves true sciences, including natural sciences, as the intellectual kinsmen of faith." The miracle of Balaam's ass, who entered into an argument with a prophet, could not be disproved even from the point of view of natural science. "Isn't it a fact, for instance, that parrots and even canary-birds can talk?" This argument by the archbishop Nikanor occupied my mind for several days, even in my dreams.

The investigations of devils and their chief, the Prince of Darkness, and of their dark kingdom, were constantly amazing to me, and diverted my rationalist mind with their codified stupidities of thousands of years. The exhaustive description and study of Paradise, with detailed bits about its location and inner structure, ended melancholically with: "The precise location of paradise is not known." And, at tea, at dinner, and during my walks, I repeated this sentence: "Regarding the geographical longitude of the felicitous paradise, there is no precise information." I seized on every opportunity to indulge in theological bickering with the police sergeant Miklin, a greedy, malicious fellow and an inveterate liar, who was extremely pious and well read in the holy books. He used to hum hymns as he hurried from cell to cell, his dangling keys ringing out as he climbed the iron stairs.

"Only for one single word, 'Christ's mother' instead of 'God's mother,'" he instructed me, "the heretic Arius's belly burst."

"And why are the bellies of the heretics to-day still intact?" I retorted. "These are . . . these are different times," he replied, in an offended tone.

Through my sister, who had come from the country, I managed to get four copies of the Bible in different languages. So I read the Gospels, verse by verse, with the help of the little knowledge of German and French that I had acquired in school, and side by side with this a parallel reading in English and Italian. In a few months, I made excellent progress in this way. I must admit, however, that my linguistic talents are very mediocre. Even now I do not know a single foreign language well, although I stayed for some time in various European countries.

For their meeting with relatives, the prisoners were transferred to narrow wooden cages separated from the visitors by a double grating. When my father came to see me for the first time, he imagined that I was always kept in that narrow box and was so overcome at the thought that he could not speak. In answer to my questions, he only moved his bloodless lips in silence. Never will I forget his face. My mother came forewarned, and was much calmer.

Echoes of what was taking place in the outside world reached us in bits. The South African war hardly touched us. We were still provincials in the full sense of the word. We were inclined to interpret the struggle between the Boers and the English chiefly as an instance of the inevitable victory of large capital over small. The Dreyfus case, which was then at its climax, thrilled us by its drama. Once a rumor reached us that a *coup d'état* had been carried out in France and that monarchy had been restored. We all felt deeply ashamed. The guards went rushing through the iron corridors and up and down the staircases trying to stop our banging and shouting. They thought we had been served inedible food. But no! It was the political wing of the prison protesting excitedly against the restoration of monarchy in France.

The articles dealing with freemasonry in the theological magazines aroused my interest. Where did this strange movement come from? I asked myself. How would Marxism explain it? I resisted the theory of historical materialism for quite a long time, and held to that of the multiplicity of historical factors, which, as we know, even to-day is the most widely accepted theory in social science. People denote as "factors" the various aspects of their social activity, endow this concept with a supra-social character, and then superstitiously interpret their own activity as the result of the interaction of these independent forces. Where did the factors come from, that is, under the influence of what conditions did they evolve from primitive human society? With these questions, the official eclectic theory does not concern itself.

It was in my cell that I read with delight two well-known essays by an old Italian Hegelian-Marxist, Antonio Labriola, which reached the prison in a French translation. Unlike most Latin writers, Labriola had mastered the materialist dialectics, if not in politics—in which he was helpless—at least in the philosophy of history. The brilliant dilettantism of his exposition actually concealed a very profound insight. He made short work, and in marvellous style, of the theory of multiple factors which were supposed to dwell on the Olympus of history and rule our fates from there.

Although thirty years have gone by since I read his essays, the general trend of his argument is still firmly intrenched in my memory, together with his continuous refrain of "ideas do not drop from the sky." After Labriola, all the Russian proponents of the multiplicity of factors, Lavrov, Mikhaylovsky, Kareyev, and others, seemed utterly ineffectual to me. Many years later I was wholly at a loss to understand some of the Marxists who had succumbed to the influence of the sterile treatise on "Economics and the Law," written by the German professor, Stammler. It was just another of the innumerable attempts to force the great stream of natural and human history, from the amœba to present-day man and beyond, through the closed rings of the eternal categories—rings which have reality only as marks on the brain of a pedant.

It was during that period that I became interested in free-masonry. For several months, I avidly studied books on its history, books given to me by relatives and friends in the town. Why had the merchants, artists, bankers, officials, and lawyers, from the first quarter of the seventeenth century on, begun to call themselves masons and tried to recreate the ritual of the mediæval guilds? What was all this strange masquerade about? Gradually the picture grew clearer. The old guild was more than a producing organization; it regulated the ethics and mode of life of its members as well. It completely embraced the life of the urban population, especially the guilds of semi-artisans and semi-artists of the building trades. The break-up of the guild system brought a moral crisis in a society which had barely emerged from mediævalism. The new morality was taking shape much more slowly than the old was being cut down. Hence, the attempt, so common in history, to preserve a form of moral discipline when its social foundations, which in this instance were those of the industrial guilds, had long since been undermined by the processes of history. Active masonry became theoretical masonry. But the old moral ways of living, which men were trying to keep just for the sake of keeping them, acquired a new meaning. In certain branches of freemasonry, elements of an obvious reactionary feudalism were prominent, as in the Scottish system. In the eighteenth century, freemasonry became expressive of a militant policy of enlightenment, as in the case of the Illuminati, who were the forerunners of revolution; on its left, it culminated in the Carbonari. Freemasons counted among their members both Louis XVI and the Dr. Guillotin who invented the guillotine. In southern Germany, freemasonry assumed an openly revolutionary character, whereas at the court of Catherine the Great it was a masquerade reflecting the aristocratic and bureaucratic hierarchy. A freemason Novikov was exiled to Siberia by a freemason empress.

Although in our day of cheap and ready-made clothing hardly anybody is still wearing his grandfather's *surtout,* in the world of ideas the *surtout* and the crinoline are still in fashion. Ideas are handed down from generation to generation, although, like grandmother's pillows and covers, they reek of staleness. Even those who are obliged to change the substance of their opinions force them into ancient moulds. The revolution in industry has been much more far-reaching than it has in ideas, where piece-work is preferred to new structures. That is why the French parliamentarians of the petty *bourgeoisie* could find no better way of creating moral ties to hold the people together against the disruptiveness of modern relations than to put on white aprons and arm themselves with a pair of compasses or a plumb-line. They were really thinking less of erecting a new building than of finding their way back into the old one of parliament or ministry.

As the prison rules demanded that a prisoner give up his old exercise-book when he was given a new one, I got for my studies on freemasonry an exercise-book with a thousand numbered pages, and entered in it, in tiny characters, excerpts from many books, interspersed with my own reflections on freemasonry, as well as on the materialist conception of history. This took up the better part of a year. I edited each chapter carefully, copied it into a note-book which had been smuggled in to me, and then sent that out to friends in other cells to read. For contriving this, we had a complicated system which we called the "telephone." The person for whom the package was intended—that is, if his cell was not too far away—would attach a weight to a piece of string, and then, holding his hand as far as he could out of the window, would swing the weight in a circle. As previously arranged through tapping, I would stick my broom out so that the weight could swing around it. Then I would draw the broom in and tie the manuscript to the string. When the person to whom I wanted to send it was too far away, we managed it by a series of stages, which of course made things more complicated.

Toward the end of my stay in the Odessa prison, the fat exercise-book, protected by the signature of the senior police sergeant, Usov, had become a veritable well of historical erudition and philosophic thought. I don't know whether it could be printed to-day as I wrote it then. I was learning too much at a time, from too many different spheres, epochs, and countries, and I am afraid that I was too anxious to tell everything at once in my first work. But I think that its main ideas and conclusions were correct. I felt, even at that time, that I was standing firmly on my own feet, and as the work progressed,

I had the feeling even more strongly. I would give a great deal to-day to find that manuscript. It went with me into exile, although there I discontinued my work on freemasonry to take up the study of Marxian economics. After my escape abroad, Alexandra Lvovna* forwarded the script to me from Siberia, through my parents, when they visited me in Paris in 1903. Later on, when I went on a secret mission to Russia, it was left in Geneva with the rest of my modest émigré archives, to become part of the *Iskra's* archives and to find there an untimely grave. After my second escape from Siberia, I tried to recover it, but in vain. Apparently it had been used to light fires or some such thing by the Swiss landlady who had been intrusted with the custody of the archives. I can't refrain here from conveying my reproaches to that worthy woman.

The way in which my work on freemasonry had to be carried on, in prison, where literary resources at my disposal were of course very limited, served me in good stead. At that time I was still comparatively ignorant of the basic literature of the Marxists. The essays by Labriola were really philosophic pamphlets and presumed a knowledge that I didn't have, and for which I had to substitute guesswork. I finished them with a bunch of hypotheses in my head. The work on freemasonry acted as a test for these hypotheses. I made no new discoveries; all the methodological conclusions at which I had arrived had been made long ago and were being applied in practice. But I groped my way to them, and somewhat independently. I think this influenced the whole course of my subsequent intellectual development. In the writings of Marx, Engels, Plekhanov and Mehring, I later found confirmation for what in prison seemed to me only a guess needing verification and theoretical justification. I did not absorb historical materialism at once, dogmatically. The dialectic method revealed itself to me for the first time not as abstract definitions but as a living spring which I had found in the historical process as I tried to understand it.

Meanwhile, the tide of revolution was beginning to rise all through the country. The historical dialectics were also working marvellously there, only in a practical sense, and on a huge

* Alexandra Lvovna Sokolovskaya, who was exiled to Siberia with the author, and became his wife.— *Translator*.

scale. The student movement vented itself in demonstrations. The Cossacks knouted the students. The liberals were indignant at this treatment of their sons. The Social Democracy was getting stronger, and was becoming an integral part of the labor movement. Revolution was no longer a privileged avocation in intellectual circles. The number of workers arrested was increasing. It was easier to breathe in the prisons, despite the overcrowding. By the end of the second year, the verdict in the case of the South Russian Workers' Union was announced: the four principal defendants were sentenced to exile in eastern Siberia for four years. After this we were still kept for over six months in the Moscow transfer prison. I used the interim for intensive studies in theory. Then for the first time I heard of Lenin, and studied his book on the development of Russian capitalism, which had just appeared, from cover to cover. Then I wrote and smuggled out of prison a pamphlet on the labor movement at Nikolayev, which was published soon after that in Geneva. We were sent away from the Moscow prison in the summer. There were interludes in other prisons. It wasn't until the autumn of 1900 that we reached our place of banishment.

CHAPTER IX

MY FIRST EXILE

WE were going down the river Lena, a few barges of convicts with a convoy of soldiers, drifting slowly along with the current. It was cold at night, and the heavy coats with which we covered ourselves were thick with frost in the morning. All along the way, at villages decided on beforehand, one or two convicts were put ashore. As well as I can remember, it took about three weeks before we came to the village of Ust-Kut. There I was put ashore with one of the woman prisoners, a close associate of mine from Nikolayev. Alexandra Lvovna had one of the most important positions in the South Russian Workers' Union. Her utter loyalty to socialism and her complete lack of any personal ambition gave her an unquestioned moral authority. The work that we were doing bound us closely together, and so, to avoid being separated, we had been married in the transfer prison in Moscow.

The village comprised about a hundred peasant huts. We settled down in one of them, on the very edge of the village. About us were the woods; below us, the river. Farther north, down the Lena, there were gold-mines. The reflection of the gold seemed to hover about the river. Ust-Kut had known lusher times, days of wild debauches, robberies, and murders. When we were there the village was very quiet, but there was still plenty of drunkenness. The couple who owned the hut that we took were inveterate tipplers. Life was dark and repressed, utterly remote from the rest of the world. At night, the cockroaches filled the house with their rustlings as they crawled over table and bed, and even over our faces. From time to time we had to move out of the hut for a day or so and keep the door wide open, at a temperature of 35 degrees (Fahrenheit) below zero.

In the summer our lives were made wretched by midges. They even bit to death a cow which had lost its way in the woods. The peasants wore nets of tarred horsehair over their heads. In the spring and autumn the village was buried in mud. To be sure, the country was beautiful, but during those years it left me cold. I hated to waste interest and time on it. I lived between the woods and the river, and I almost never noticed them—I was so busy with my books and personal relations. I was studying Marx, brushing the cockroaches off the page.

The Lena was the great water route of the exiled. Those who had completed their terms returned to the South by way of the river. But communication was continuous between these various nests of the banished which kept growing with the rise of the revolutionary tide. The exiles exchanged letters with each other, some of them so long that they were really theoretical treatises. It was comparatively easy to get a transfer from one place to another from the governor of Irkutsk. Alexandra Lvovna and I moved to a place 250 versts east on the river Ilim, where we had friends. I found a job there, for a while, as clerk to a millionaire merchant. His fur depots, stores and saloons were scattered over a territory as big as Belgium and Holland put together. He was a powerful merchant-lord. He referred to the thousands of Tunguses under him as "my little Tunguses." He couldn't even write his name; he had to mark it with a cross. He lived in niggardly fashion the whole year round, and then would squander tens of thousands of roubles at the annual fair at Nijni-Novgorod. I worked under him for a month and a half. Then one day I entered on a bill a pound of red-lead as "one pood" (forty pounds), and sent this huge bill to a distant store. This completely ruined my reputation with my employer, and I was discharged.

So we went back to Ust-Kut. The cold was terrific; the temperature dropped as low as 55 degrees (Fahrenheit) below zero. The coachman had to break the icicles off the horses' muzzles as we drove along. I held a ten-months-old baby-girl on my knees. We had made a fur funnel to put over her head, arranged so that she could breathe through it and at every stop we removed her fearfully from her coverings, to see if she was still alive. Nothing untoward happened on that trip, however. We didn't stay long at Ust-Kut. After a few months, the governor gave us permission to move a little farther south, to a place called Verkholensk, where we had friends.

The aristocracy among the exiles was made up of the old Populists who had more or less succeeded in establishing themselves during the long years they had been away. The young Marxists formed a distinct section by themselves. It was not until my time that the striking workers, often illiterates who by some freak of fate had been separated from the great mass, began to drift to the north. For them, exile proved an invaluable school for politics and general culture. Intellectual disagreements were made the more bitter by squabbles over personal matters, as is natural where a great many people are forcibly confined. Private, and especially romantic, conflicts frequently took on the proportions of drama. There were even suicides on this account. At Verkholensk, we took turns at guarding a student from Kiev. I noticed a pile of shining metal shavings on his table. We found out later that he had made lead bullets for his shotgun. Our guarding him was in vain. With the barrel of the gun against his breast, he pulled the trigger with his foot. We buried him in silence on the hill. At that time, we were still shy about making speeches, as if there were something artificial about them. In all the big exile colonies, there were graves of suicides. Some of the exiles became absorbed into the local populations, especially in the towns; others took to drink. In exile, as in prison, only hard intellectual work could save one. The Marxists, I must admit, were the only ones who did any of it under these conditions.

It was on the great Lena route, at that time, that I met Dzerzhinsky, Uritzky, and other young revolutionaries who were destined to play such important rôles in the future. We awaited each arriving party eagerly. On a dark spring night, as we sat around a bonfire on the banks of the Lena, Dzerzhinsky read one of his poems, in Polish. His face and voice were beautiful, but the poem was a slight thing. The life of the man was to prove to be one of the sternest of poems.

Soon after our arrival at Ust-Kut, I began to contribute articles to an Irkutsk newspaper, the *Vostochnoye Obozreniye* (*The Eastern Review*). It was a provincial organ within the law, started by the old Populist exiles, but occasionally it fell into the hands of Marxists. I began as a village correspondent, and I waited anxiously for my first article to appear. The editor encouraged my contributions, and I soon began to write about literature, as well as about public questions. One day when I was trying to think of a pen-name, I opened the Italian dictionary and "antidoto" was the first word that met my eye. So for several years I signed myself "Antid Oto," and jestingly explained to my friends that I wanted to inject the Marxist antidote into the legitimate newspapers. After a while, my pay jumped suddenly from two kopecks a line to four. It was the best proof of success. I wrote about the peasantry; about the Russian classic authors; about Ibsen, Hauptmann and Nietzsche; de Maupassant, Andreyev and Gorky. I sat up night after night scratching up my manuscripts, as I tried to find the exact idea or the right word to express it. I was becoming a writer.

Since 1896, when I had tried to ward off revolutionary ideas, and the following year, when I had done the same to Marxist doctrines even though I was already carrying on revolutionary work, I had travelled far. At the time of my exile, Marxism had definitely become the basis of my philosophy. During the exile, I tried to consider, from the new point of view I had acquired, the so-called "eternal" problems of life: love, death, friendship, optimism, pessimism, and so forth. In different epochs, and in varying social surroundings, man loves and hates and hopes differently. Just as the tree feeds its leaves, flowers, and fruits with the extracts absorbed from the soil by its roots, so does the individual find food for his sentiment and ideas, even the most "sublime" ones, in the economic roots of society. In my literary articles written in this period, I developed virtually one theme only: the relations between the individual and society. Not very long ago, these articles were published in a single volume, and when I saw them collected I realized that although I might have written them differently to-day, I should not have had to change the substance of them.

At that time, official or so-called "legal" Russian Marxism was in the throes of a crisis. I could see then from actual experience how brazenly new social requirements create for themselves intellectual garments from the cloth of a theory that was intended for something quite different. Until the nineties, the greater part of the Russian intelligentsia was stagnating in Populist theories with their rejection of capitalist development and idealization of peasant communal ownership of the land.

And capitalism in the meantime was holding out to the intelligentsia the promise of all sorts of material blessings and political influence. The sharp knife of Marxism was the instrument by which the bourgeois intelligentsia cut the Populist umbilical cord, and severed itself from a hated past. It was this that accounted for the swift and victorious spread of Marxism during the latter years of the last century.

As soon as Marxism had accomplished this, however, it began to irk this same intelligentsia. Its dialectics were convenient for demonstrating the progress of capitalist methods of development, but finding that it led to a revolutionary rejection of the whole capitalist system, they adjudged it an impediment and declared it out of date. At the turn of the century, at the time when I was in prison and exile, the Russian intelligentsia was going through a phase of wide-spread criticism of Marxism. They accepted its historical justification of capitalism, but discarded its rejection of capitalism by revolutionary means. In this roundabout way the old Populist intelligentsia, with its archaic sympathies, was slowly being transformed into a liberal bourgeois intelligentsia.

European criticisms of Marxism now found a ready hearing in Russia, irrespective of their quality. It is enough to say that Eduard Bernstein became one of the most popular guides from socialism to liberalism. The normative philosophy, shouting victory with more and more assurance, was ousting the materialist dialectics. Bourgeois public opinion, in its formative stages, needed inflexible norms, not only to protect it against the tyrannies of the autocratic bureaucracy, but against the wild revolutionism of the masses. Kant, although he overthrew Hegel, did not in turn hold his position very long. Russian liberalism came very late, and from the first lived on volcanic soil. The categorical imperative, it found, gave it too abstract and unreliable a security. Much stronger measures were needed to resist the revolutionary masses. The transcendental idealists became orthodox Christians. Bulgakov, a professor of political economy, began with a revision of Marxism on the agrarian question, went on to idealism, and ended by becoming a priest. But this last stage was not reached until some years later.

In the early years of this century, Russia was a vast laboratory of social thinking. My work on the history of freemasonry had fortified me in a realization of the subordinate place of ideas in the historical process. "Ideas do not drop from the sky," I repeated after old Labriola. Now it was no longer a question of pure scientific study, but of the choice of a political path. The revision of Marxism that was going on in all directions helped me as it did many another young Marxist—it helped us to make up our minds and sharpen our weapons. We needed Marxism, not only to rid ourselves of Populism, which touched us but slightly, but actually to begin a stout war against capitalism in its own territory. The struggles against the Revisionists toughened us politically, as well as in the field of theory. We were becoming proletarian revolutionaries.

During this same period, we met with a great deal of criticism from our left. In one of the northern colonies—I think it was Viluysk—lived an exile called Makhaisky, whose name soon became generally known. Makhaisky began as a critic of Social Democratic opportunism. His first hectographed essay, devoted to an exposure of the opportunism of the German Social Democracy, had a great vogue among the exiles. His second essay criticised the economic system of Marx and ended with the amazing conclusion that Socialism is a social order based on the exploitation of the workers by a professional intelligentsia. The third essay advocated the rejection of political struggle, in the spirit of anarchist syndicalism. For several months, the work of Makhaisky held first place in the interest of the Lena exiles. It gave me a powerful inoculation against anarchism, a theory very sweeping in its verbal negations, but lifeless and cowardly in its practical conclusions.

The first time I ever met a living anarchist was in the Moscow transfer prison. He was a village school-teacher, Luzin, a man reserved and uncommunicative, even cruel. In prison he always preferred to be with the criminals and would listen intently to their tales of robbery and murder. He avoided discussions of theory. But once when I pressed him to tell me how railways would be managed by autonomous communities, he answered: "Why the hell should I want to travel on railways under anarchism?" That answer was enough for me. Luzin tried to win the workers over, and we carried on a concealed warfare which was not devoid of hostility.

We made the journey to Siberia together. During the high floods on the river, Luzin decided to cross the Lena in a boat. He was not quite sober and challenged me to go with him. I agreed. Loose timber and dead animals were floating on the surface of the swollen river; there were many whirlpools. We made the crossing safely, though not without exciting moments. Luzin gave me a sort of verbal testimonial: a "good comrade," or something to that effect, and we became friendlier. Soon after, however, he was transferred to a place farther north. A few months later he stabbed the local police-chief with a knife. The policeman was not a bad sort of fellow and the wound did not prove dangerous. At the trial Luzin declared that he had nothing against the man personally, but that he wanted, through him, to strike at the tyranny of the state. He was sentenced to hard-labor.

While hot discussions were seething in the far-flung, snow-covered Siberian exile colonies—discussions of such things as the differentiation of the Russian peasantry, the English trades-unions, the relationship between the categorical imperative and the class interests, and between Marxism and Darwinism—a struggle of a special sort was taking place in government spheres. In February, 1901, the Holy Synod excommunicated Leo Tolstoy.

The edict was published in all the papers. Tolstoy was accused of six crimes: 1. "He rejects the personal, living God, glorified in the Holy Trinity." 2. "He denies Christ as the God-man risen from the dead." 3. "He denies the Immaculate Conception and the virginity, before and after the birth, of the God-mother." 4. "He does not recognize life after death and retribution for sins." 5. "He rejects the benefaction of the Holy Ghost." 6. "He mocks at the sacrament of the Eucharist." The gray-bearded metropolitans, Pobedonostzev, who was inspiring them, and all the other pillars of the state who looked upon us revolutionaries as half-mad fanatics, not to say criminals—whereas they, in their own eyes, were the representatives of sober thought based on the historical experience of man—it was these people who demanded that the great artist-realist subscribe to the faith in the Immaculate Conception, and in the transubstantiation of the Holy Ghost through wafers. We read the list of Tolstoy's heresies over and

over again, each time with fresh astonishment, and said to ourselves: No, it is we who rest on the experience of man, it is
we who represent the future, while those men at the top are
not merely criminals but maniacs as well. We were absolutely
sure that we would get the better of that lunatic asylum.

The old structure of the state was cracking all through its
foundations. The students were still the ringleaders in the
struggle, and in their impatience began to employ the methods
of terrorism. After the shots fired by Karpovich and Balmashov,* all the exiles were as much aroused as if they had heard
the bugle-call of alarm. Arguments about the use of terrorist
methods began. After individual vacillations, the Marxist section of the exiled went on record against terrorism. The chem-
istry of high explosives cannot take the place of mass action,
we said. Individuals may be destroyed in a heroic struggle, but
that will not rouse the working class to action. Our task is
not the assassination of the Czar's ministers, but the revolutionary overthrow of Czarism. This is where the line was
drawn between the Social Democrats and the Socialist-Revolutionists. While my theoretical views were formed in prison,
my political self-determination was achieved in exile.

Two years had passed in this way, and much water had
flowed under the bridges of St. Petersburg, Moscow, and War-
saw. A movement begun underground was now walking the
streets of the cities. In some districts, the peasantry was beginning to stir. Social Democratic organizations sprang up
even in Siberia, along the line of the Trans-Siberian railway.
They got in touch with me, and I wrote proclamations and
leaflets for them. After a three years' interval, I was rejoining
the ranks for active struggle.

The exiles were no longer willing to stay in their places of
confinement, and there was an epidemic of escapes. We had to
arrange a system of rotation. In almost every village there
were individual peasants who as youths had come under the
influence of the older generation of revolutionaries. They
would carry the "politicals" away secretly in boats, in carts, or
on sledges, and pass them along from one to another. The
police in Siberia were as helpless as we were. The vastness of

---

* Karpovich shot Bogolyepov, Minister of Education, in 1901. Balmashov
shot Sipyagin, Minister of the Interior, in 1902.—*Translator.*

the country was an ally, but an enemy as well. It was very hard to catch a runaway, but the chances were that he would be drowned in the river or frozen to death in the primeval forests.

The revolutionary movement had spread far and wide, but it still lacked unity. Every district and every town was carrying on its individual struggle. Czarism had the invaluable advantage of concerted action. The necessity for creating a centralized party was engaging the minds of many revolutionaries. I devoted an essay to this, and copies of it were circulated throughout the colonies; it was discussed with avidity. It seemed to us that our fellow Social Democrats in Russia and abroad were not giving this question enough thought. But they did think and act. In the summer of 1902, I received, by way of Irkutsk, a number of books in the binding of which were concealed the latest publications from abroad, printed on extremely fine paper. We learned from them that there was a Marxian newspaper published abroad, the *Iskra,* which had as its object the creation of a centralized organization of professional revolutionaries who would be bound together by the iron discipline of action. A book by Lenin also reached us, a book published in Geneva, entitled "What Is to Be Done?" which dealt exclusively with the same problem. My hand-written essays, newspaper articles, and proclamations for the Siberian Union immediately looked small and provincial to me in the face of the new and tremendous task which confronted us. I had to look for another field of activity. I had to escape from exile.

At that time we already had two daughters. The younger was four months old. Life under conditions in Siberia was not easy, and my escape would place a double burden on the shoulders of Alexandra Lvovna. But she met this objection with the two words: "You must." Duty to the revolution overshadowed everything else for her, personal considerations especially. She was the first to broach the idea of my escape when we realized the great new tasks. She brushed away all my doubts.

For several days after I had escaped, she concealed my absence from the police. From abroad, I could hardly keep up a correspondence with her. Then she was exiled for a second time; after this we met only occasionally. Life separated us, but nothing could destroy our friendship and our intellectual kinship.

CHAPTER X

MY FIRST ESCAPE

AUTUMN was drawing near, with its threat of impassable roads. To speed my escape, we decided to kill two birds with one stone. A peasant friend agreed to drive me out of Verkholensk, together with E. G., a woman translator of Marx. At night, in the fields, he hid us under hay and matting in his cart, as if we were mere cargo. At the same time, to ward off the suspicions of the police, they kept a dummy of a supposedly sick man in the bed in my house for a few days. The driver sped on in the Siberian fashion, making as much as twenty versts an hour. I counted all the bumps with my back, to the accompaniment of the groans of my companion. During the trip the horses were changed twice. Before we reached the railway, my companion and I went our separate ways, so that each of us would not have to suffer the mishaps and risks incurred by the other. I got into the railway-carriage in safety. There my friends from Irkutsk provided me with a travelling-case filled with starched shirts, neckties and other attributes of civilization. In my hands, I had a copy of the "Iliad" in the Russian hexameter of Gnyeditch; in my pocket, a passport made out in the name of Trotsky, which I wrote in it at random, without even imagining that it would become my name for the rest of my life. I was following the Siberian line toward the West. The station police let me pass with indifference.

At the stations along the way the tall Siberian women sold roast chickens and suckling pigs, bottled milk and great heaps of bread. Every one of the stations was like an exhibition of Siberian produce. Throughout the journey, the entire car full of passengers drank tea and ate cheap Siberian buns. I read the hexameter and dreamed of the life abroad. The escape proved to be quite without romantic glamour; it dissolved into nothing but an endless drinking of tea.

I made a halt at Samara, where the interior general staff of the *Iskra*, as distinct from the foreign-émigré staff, was concentrated. At the head of it was a certain Kler, the name which the engineer Krzhizhanovsky, who is the present chairman of the State Planning Committee, had assumed as a disguise. He and his wife were friends of Lenin, and had been associated with him in the Social Democratic work in St. Petersburg in the years of 1894–5, and in the exile in Siberia. After the defeat of the revolution in 1905, Kler, together with many other thousands of revolutionists, withdrew from the party, and as an engineer achieved an important place in the industrial world. The revolutionaries, who continued to work in secret, complained that he refused to give such help as even the liberals had given earlier. After an interval of from ten to twelve years, Krzhizhanovsky rejoined the party, after it had already come into power. This was the course of many of the intelligentsia who are the backbone of Stalin's régime to-day.

In Samara, I joined—officially, as it were—the *Iskra* organization under the name of Pero (pen), assigned to me by Kler as a tribute to my successes as a journalist in Siberia. The organization was building up the party all over again. The first party congress, held in Minsk in 1898, had failed to establish a centralized party. Wholesale arrests destroyed an incipient organization which was not rooted firmly enough throughout the country. After this, the revolutionary movement continued to grow in scattered centres, maintaining its provincial character. Simultaneously, its intellectual level showed signs of lowering. The Social Democrats, in their effort to win the masses, let their political slogans recede into the background. And thus the so-called "Economic" school of Social Democratic policy was evolved. It drew its strength from the industrial boom and the preponderance of strikes. Toward the end of the century, a crisis developed that accentuated the antagonisms all over the country, and gave the political movement a strong impetus. The *Iskra* launched a militant campaign against the provincial "Economists," and advocated a centralized revolutionary party. The general staff of the *Iskra* was established abroad, so that the organization, which was being carefully recruited from among the so-called "professional" revolutionaries, would be assured of an ideological stability, and would be bound together by unity in theory and in practical method. At the same time, most of the adherents of the

Iskra still belonged to the intelligentsia. They fought for the control over local Social Democratic committees, and for a party congress which would insure a victory for the ideas and methods of the *Iskra*. This was really a draft outline of the revolutionary organization, which, as it developed and hardened, advanced and retreated, became more and more closely bound to the masses of workers, set before them ever more far-reaching tasks, and fifteen years later overthrew the *bourgeoisie* and assumed power.

At the request of the Samara organization, I visited Kharkoff, Poltava and Kiev, to meet a number of revolutionaries who had already joined the *Iskra* or who had still to be won over. I returned to Samara with little accomplished; the connections with the South were still very ineffectual; in Kharkoff the address given me proved false, and in Poltava I ran into a sort of local patriotism. It was obvious that a single trip to the provinces could achieve nothing; it was persistent work that was needed. Meanwhile Lenin, with whom the Samara bureau kept up a lively correspondence, urged me to hasten my departure for abroad. Kler supplied me with the money for the trip, and the necessary information for crossing the Austrian frontier near Kamenetz-Podolsk.

A whole train of adventures more amusing than tragic began at the station at Samara. To avoid meeting the station-police a second time, I decided to board the train at the last possible moment. My seat was to be held for me and my travelling-bag brought to the railway-carriage by a student named Solovyov, who is to-day one of the heads of the Oil Syndicate. I was walking peacefully back and forth in the field far away from the station, keeping my eye on the clock, when I suddenly heard the second bell. I realized that I had been given the wrong time for the departure of the train, and dashed to the station for all I was worth. Solovyov, who had been waiting for me in the car, as he had promised, and had to jump off the train after it had begun to move, was standing surrounded by the station-police and officials. The sight of a breathless man arriving post-haste after the train had started attracted general attention. The police threatened to take action against Solovyov, but it only ended in sarcastic jokes at our expense.

I reached the frontier zone without any trouble. At the last station the policeman asked for my passport. I was genuinely surprised when he found the paper that I had fabricated myself perfectly in order. A boy who was studying at the *gymnasium* had charge of smuggling me across the frontier. He is now a prominent chemist at the head of one of the science institutes of the Soviet Republic. In his political views he favored the Socialist-Revolutionists. When he heard that I belonged to the *Iskra* organization, he said: "Do you know that *Iskra*, in its last issues, has been engaging in shameful polemics against terrorism?"

I was about to begin a theoretical discussion when the young fellow added with a great show of temper: "I won't conduct you across the frontier." This argument amazed me because it was so unexpected. And yet it was perfectly legitimate. Fifteen years later we had to fight the power of the Socialist-Revolutionists with arms in hand. At that moment, however, I was not interested in historical prospects. I argued that it was not fair to punish me for an article in the *Iskra*, and finally declared that I would not budge until I had obtained a guide. The boy relented. "Well," he said, "I will help you. But tell them over there that this is the last time."

The fellow put me up for the night in the empty house of a commercial traveller who was to return the next day. I remember vaguely that I had to make my way into the locked house through a window. At night I was awakened suddenly by a flash of light. A strange little man in a bowler hat was bending over me with a candle in one hand and a stick in the other. From the ceiling, a huge shadow of a man was crawling toward me. "Who are you?" I asked indignantly. "I like that!" answered the stranger. "He is lying in my bed and asks me who I am!" Obviously, this was the owner of the house. My attempt to explain to him that he wasn't supposed to return until the next day made not the slightest impression on him. "I know when I am supposed to return," he rejoined, not unreasonably. The situation was getting complicated. "I understand," exclaimed the host. "This is one of Alexander's little jokes. But I shall talk it over with him to-morrow." I readily chimed in with his happy thought that the cause of all the trouble was the absent Alexander. I spent the rest of the night with the commercial traveller, who even graciously treated me to tea.

Next morning, the student at the *gymnasium,* after a stormy time of explaining everything to my host, handed me over to the smugglers of the village of Brody. I whiled away the day in a barn, while its owner, a Ukrainian peasant, fed me liberally on watermelons. At night, in a rain-storm, he led me across the frontier. For a long time we had to wade in the dark, stumbling every now and then. "Now, get on my back," said my guide, "there is water farther on." I protested. "You can't possibly appear on the other side all wet," he insisted. So I had to continue the journey on the man's back, which didn't save me, however, from getting water in my shoes.

About a quarter of an hour later we were drying ourselves out in a Jewish hut in the Austrian section of Brody. The people there informed me that the guide had purposely led me into deep water to get more money from me. For his part, the Ukrainian, as he was taking his leave, warned me in a friendly way against the Jews, who always like to make one pay three times more than one owes them. And, indeed, my resources were swiftly melting away. I still had another eight kilometres to make before I could reach the railway-station. For one or two kilometres along the frontier, on a road whipped into mud by the rain, until we reached the main road, the going was not only difficult, but dangerous as well. I was riding in a little two-wheeled cart with an old Jewish workman for a driver.

"One day I shall lose my life in this business," he muttered.

"Why?"

"Because soldiers keep calling out and if you don't answer them, they shoot. You can see their light over there. Fortunately, this is a fine night."

The night was fine indeed! A cutting and impenetrable autumn darkness, an interminable rain hitting one in the face, and mud sloshing under the horse's hoofs. We were going up-hill; the wheels kept slipping; the old man was cajoling the horse in a gruff half-whisper; the wheels sank, the light cart tilted more and more, and suddenly went right over. The October mud was cold and deep. I fell down flat, sinking half into it. And to top it all, I lost my glasses. But the most awful thing was that just after we had fallen, there was a terrible piercing cry, right where we were, at our very side, a cry of despair, imploring help—a mystic appeal to heaven. It was beyond the power of reason to say, in that dark, wet night, to whom that mysterious voice belonged—a voice so expressive and yet not human.

"I tell you, he will ruin us," muttered the old man in despair. "He will ruin us!"

"Who is it?" I asked, almost afraid to breathe.

"It's the rooster, curse him, the rooster that my mistress gave me to take to the rabbi to have killed for Saturday." The penetrating shrieks continued at regular intervals. "He will ruin us. It's only two hundred steps to the post; the soldiers will rush out in a moment."

"Strangle him," I hissed in a rage.

"Who? The rooster? Where am I to find him? He must have got pinned under something!"

We both crawled around in the dark and grubbed in the mud with our hands, while the rain lashed us from above. We cursed the rooster and our fate. Finally, the old man freed the miserable sufferer from under my blanket, and the grateful bird immediately stopped crying. We lifted the cart together, and continued our journey. At the station, I spent three hours drying out and cleaning myself up before the train arrived.

After I had changed my money, I found that I shouldn't have enough to reach my destination, which was Zurich, where I was to present myself to Axelrod. I bought a ticket to Vienna, and decided that there I would arrange for the next lap.

Vienna surprised me most of all by the fact that I could understand no one, despite my study of German at school. Most of the passers-by found me equally difficult. Nevertheless, I managed finally to tell an old man in a red cap that I wanted to get to the offices of the *Arbeiter-Zeitung*. I had made up my mind that I would explain to no one less than Victor Adler, the leader of the Austrian Social Democracy, that the interests of the Russian revolution demanded my immediate presence in Zurich. The guide agreed to take me there. We walked for an hour. Then we found out that two years earlier the paper had moved its offices to a new address. We walked for another half-hour. Then the doorman informed us that visiting hours were over. I had no money to pay the guide, I was hungry, and what was most important of all, I *had* to get to Zurich. A gentleman who didn't look too amiable was coming down the steps. I addressed myself to him with a query about Adler.

"Do you know what day it is?" he asked me sternly.

I did not know; in the train, in the cart, in the house of the commercial traveller, in the Ukrainian's barn, in the midnight struggle with the rooster, I had lost track of time.

"To-day is Sunday," the old gentleman announced, and tried to pass by me.

"No matter—I want to see Adler."

At this, my interrogator answered me in the voice of one giving orders to a battalion of troops in a storm: "I am telling you, Dr. Adler cannot be seen on Sundays."

"But I have important business with him," I persisted.

"Even if your business were ten times as important—do you understand?" It was Fritz Austerlitz himself speaking, the terror of his office, a man whose conversation, as Hugo would have said, consisted only of lightning. "Even if you had brought the news—you hear me?—that your Czar had been assassinated, that a revolution had broken out in your country —do you hear?—even this would not give you the right to disturb the Doctor's Sunday rest."

I was beginning to be impressed by the thunders of the gentleman's voice. All the same I thought he was talking nonsense. It was inconceivable that a Sunday's rest should be rated above the demands of revolution. I decided not to give in. I had to get to Zurich. The editors of the *Iskra* were waiting for me. Besides, I had escaped from Siberia—surely that was of some importance. Finally, by standing at the bottom of the staircase and barring the stern gentleman's way, I got what I wanted. Austerlitz gave me the address. Accompanied by the same guide, I went to Adler's house.

A short man, with a pronounced stoop, almost a hunch, and with swollen eyes in a tired face, came out to see me. At the time there was a Landtag election in Vienna. Adler had made speeches at several meetings the day before, and during the night had written his articles and exhortations. I learned all this a quarter of an hour later from his daughter-in-law.

"Pardon me for disturbing your Sunday rest, Doctor."

"Go on, go on," he said with seeming sternness, but in a tone that did not frighten but encouraged me instead. One could see intelligence emanating from each wrinkle of the man.

"I am Russian."

"You need not tell me that, I have had enough time to guess it."

I told the Doctor, while he studied me with swift glances, about my conversation at the entrance to his office.

"Is that so? Did they tell you that? Who could it have been? A tall man? Shouts? Oh, that was Austerlitz. You said he shouted? Oh, yes, it was Austerlitz. Don't take it too seriously. If you ever bring news of a revolution in Russia, you may ring my bell, even at night. Katya, Katya," he called out suddenly. His Russian daughter-in-law came out. "Now we shall get along better," he said, leaving us.

My further travel was assured.

CHAPTER XI

AN ÉMIGRÉ FOR THE FIRST TIME

I ARRIVED in London from Zurich by way of Paris, in the autumn of 1902. I think it was in October, early in the morning, when a cab, engaged after I had resorted to all sorts of pantomime, drove me to the address written on a slip of paper. My destination was Lenin's house. I had been instructed before I left Zurich to knock on the door three times. The door was opened by Nadyezhda Konstantinovna, who had probably been wakened by my knocking. It was early, and any one used to civilized ways would have waited quietly at the station for an hour or two, instead of knocking at the door of a strange house at such an unearthly hour. But I was still impelled by the force that had set me off on my journey from Verkholensk. I had disturbed Axelrod in Zurich in the same barbarous way, although that was in the middle of the night, instead of at dawn. Lenin was still in bed, and the kindly expression of his face was tinged with a justifiable amazement. Such was the setting for our first meeting and conversation. Both Vladimir Ilyich* and Nadyezhda Konstantinovna already knew of me from Kler's letter, and had been waiting for me.

I was greeted with: "The Pero has arrived!" At once I unloaded my modest list of impressions of Russia: the connections in the South are bad, the secret *Iskra* address in Kharkov is wrong, the editors of the *Southern Worker* oppose amalgamation, the crossing at the Austrian frontier is in the hands of a student at the *gymnasium* who refuses help to followers of the *Iskra*. The facts in themselves were not of a sort to fill one with much hope, but there was faith enough to make up for it, and to spare.

*Lenin's full original name name is Vladimir Ilyich Ulyanov, Nikolay Lenin being his party- and pen-name. Since the revolution it has become customary to refer to him as Vladimir Ilyich Lenin, and more familiarly as Ilyich. His wife's maiden name is Nadyezhda Konstantinovna Krupskaya.—*Translator*.

Either the same or the next morning, Vladimir Ilyich and I went for a long walk around London. From a bridge, Lenin pointed out Westminster and some other famous buildings. I don't remember the exact words he used, but what he conveyed was: "This is their famous Westminster," and "their" referred of course not to the English but to the ruling classes. This implication, which was not in the least emphasized, but coming as it did from the very innermost depths of the man, and expressed more by the tone of his voice than by anything else, was always present, whether Lenin was speaking of the treasures of culture, of new achievements, of the wealth of books in the British Museum, of the information of the larger European newspapers, or, years later, of German artillery or French aviation. They know this or they have that, they have made this or achieved that—but what enemies they are! To his eyes, the invisible shadow of the ruling classes always overlay the whole of human culture—a shadow that was as real to him as daylight.

The architecture of London scarcely attracted my attention at that time. Transferred bodily from Verkholensk to countries beyond the Russian border which I was seeing for the first time, I absorbed Vienna, Paris and London in a most summary fashion, and details like the Westminster Palace seemed quite superfluous. It wasn't for that, of course, that Lenin had taken me out for this long walk. His object was to become acquainted with me, and to question me. His examination, it must be admitted, was very thorough indeed.

I told him all about our Siberian discussions, especially on the question of a centralized organization; about my essay on the subject; about the violent encounters I had had with the old Populists in Irkutsk, where I had stayed for a few weeks; about the three essays by Makhaysky, and so forth. Lenin knew how to listen.

"And how did you fare in questions of theory?"

I told him how we, as a group, had studied his book, "The Development of Capitalism in Russia," in the transfer-prison in Moscow, and how in exile we had worked on Marx's "Capital," but had stopped at the second volume. We had studied the controversy between Bernstein and Kautsky intently, using the original sources. There were no followers of Bernstein among us. In philosophy, we had been much impressed by Bogdanov's book, which combined Marxism with the theory of knowledge put forward by Mach and Avenarius. Lenin also thought, at the time, that Bogdanov's theories were right. "I am not a philosopher," he said, with a slightly timorous expression, "but Plekhanov denounces Bogdanov's philosophy as a disguised sort of idealism." A few years later, Lenin dedicated a big volume to the discussion of Mach and Avenarius; his criticism of their theories was fundamentally identical with that voiced by Plekhanov.

I mentioned, during our conversation, that the Siberian exiles had been greatly impressed by the enormous amount of statistical data analyzed in Lenin's book on Russian capitalism. "Well, it was not done all at once, you know," he answered, as if somewhat embarrassed. He was apparently greatly pleased that the younger comrades appreciated the tremendous amount of work he had put into his principal opus on economics. My own future work was discussed then only in a very general way. We assumed that I would stay abroad for a time, get acquainted with current literature, look around, and the rest would be discussed afterward. At any event, I intended to return illegally to Russia for revolutionary work some time later.

Nadyezhda Konstantinovna took me to a house a few blocks away, where lived Vera Zasulitch, Martov, and Blumenfeld. the *Iskra* printing-press manager, and where they found a room for me. According to the English custom, the rooms were arranged vertically, and not on the same floor, as in Russia: the lowest room was occupied by the landlady, and the lodgers had rooms one above another. There was also a common room in which we drank coffee, smoked, and engaged in endless discussions. This room, thanks chiefly to Zasulitch, but not without help from Martov, was always in a state of rank disorder. Plekhanov, after his first visit to the room, described it as a "den."

That was the beginning of my brief London episode. I took to studying the published issues of the *Iskra*, and the review of *Zarya*, which came from the same offices. These were brilliant periodicals, combining scientific profundity with revolutionary passion. I actually fell in love with the *Iskra*, and was so ashamed of my ignorance that I strained every nerve in my effort to overcome it. Soon I began to write for the *Iskra*. At first it was only short notes, but a little later I wrote political articles and even editorials.

At that time, too, I gave a public lecture in Whitechapel, when I had a passage-at-arms with the patriarch of the Russian émigrés, Tchaikovsky, and with the anarchist Tcherkezov, also a man of advanced years. I was honestly amazed at the infantile arguments with which these worthy elders were trying to crush Marxism. I returned home, I remember, as if I were walking on air. In my contacts with Whitechapel, and with the outside world in general, my go-between was an old Londoner, Alexeyev, an émigré Marxist who was closely allied with the editors of the *Iskra*. He initiated me into the mysteries of English life, and in general was my source of information on all sorts of things. Of Lenin, Alexeyev spoke with very great respect. "I believe," he said to me once, "that Lenin is more important for the revolution than Plekhanov." I did not mention this to Lenin, of course, but I did to Martov. Martov made no comment.

One Sunday I went with Lenin and Krupskaya to a Social Democratic meeting in a church, where speeches alternated with the singing of hymns. The principal speaker was a compositor who had just returned from Australia. He spoke of the Social revolution. Then everybody rose and sang: "Lord Almighty, let there be no more kings or rich men!" I could scarcely believe my eyes or ears. When we came out of the church, Lenin said: "There are many revolutionary and socialistic elements among the English proletariat, but they are mixed up with conservatism, religion, and prejudices, and can't somehow break through to the surface and unite."

After attending the Social Democratic church, we had dinner in the tiny kitchen of a two-room apartment. My friends jested as usual about my finding my way home. I was very bad at making my way about the streets and, with my usual penchant for systematic thinking, called this defect "a topographic cretinism." Later I did better in this respect, but my improvement was not won without a great deal of effort.

My modest knowledge of English acquired in the prison at Odessa was increased very little by my stay in London. I was too much absorbed in Russian affairs. British Marxism was not interesting. The intellectual centre of the Social Democracy at that time was Germany, and we watched intently the struggle then going on between the "orthodox" Marxists and the "revisionists."

In London, as well as later on in Geneva, I met Zasulitch and Martov much more often than Lenin. Since we lived in the same house in London, and in Geneva usually had our meals in the same restaurants, I was with Martov and Zasulitch several times a day, whereas Lenin led the life of a family man, and every meeting with him, aside from the official meetings, was a small event. The Bohemian habits and tastes which weighed so heavily with Martov were utterly alien to Lenin. He knew that time, be it ever so relative, was the most absolute of gifts. He spent a great deal of time in the library of the British Museum, where he carried on his theoretical studies, and where he usually wrote his newspaper articles. With his assistance, I obtained admission to that sanctuary too. I was insatiable, and simply gorged myself on the superabundance of books there. Soon, however, I had to leave for the continent.

After my "test" public appearance in Whitechapel, I was sent on a lecture tour of Brussels, Liège and Paris. My lecture was devoted to the defense of historical materialism against the criticisms of the so-called "Russian subjective school." Lenin was very much interested in my subject. I gave him my detailed synopsis to look over, and he advised me to revise the lecture so that it could be published in an article in the next issue of the *Zarya*. But I didn't have the courage to appear by the side of Plekhanov and the others with a strictly theoretical essay.

From Paris, I was soon summoned by cable to London. They were planning to smuggle me over to Russia again, as reports from there complained about wholesale arrests and the shortage of men, and demanded my return. But I had hardly set foot in London when the plan was changed. Deutsch, who lived in London then and treated me very kindly, told me afterward how he had stood up for me, urging that the "youth" (he had no other name for me) needed a stay abroad for a while to improve his education, and how Lenin had agreed with him. The prospect of working in the Russian organization of the *Iskra* was tempting, but nevertheless I was very glad to be able to stay abroad a little longer.

I returned to Paris, where, unlike London, the Russian student colony was very large. The revolutionary parties were fighting each other bitterly to win over the mass of the students. Here is an excerpt from the recollections of that period by N. I. Sedova:

"The autumn of 1902 was marked by frequent lectures in the Russian colony in Paris. The *Iskra* group, to which I belonged, saw first Martov, and then Lenin. A war was being fought against the 'Economists' and the Socialist-Revolutionists. In our group there was some talk about the arrival of a young comrade who had escaped from Siberia. He called at the house of E. M. Alexandrova, formerly one of the Narodovoltsi, who had joined the *Iskra*. We of the younger generation were very fond of Ekaterina Mikhailovna, listened to her talks with great interest, and were much under her influence. When the young contributor to the *Iskra* made his appearance in Paris, Ekaterina Mikhailovna bade me find out if there was a vacant room near by. There happened to be one in the house where I lived. The rent for it was 12 francs a month, but the room was small, dark and narrow, just like a prison cell. When I began describing the room to her, Ekaterina Mikhailovna cut me short with: 'That's enough describing— it will do. Let him take it.'

"After the young comrade (whose name was not revealed to us) established himself in the room, Ekaterina Mikhailovna asked me: 'Is he preparing for his lecture?'

" 'I don't know, I suppose so,' I answered. 'Last night as I was coming up-stairs I heard him whistling in his room.'

" 'Then tell him to work hard and not whistle.' She was very anxious that 'he' should be successful. But her anxiety was uncalled for. The lecture went off very well and the colony was delighted, as the young follower of the *Iskra* exceeded all expectations."

I was much more interested in learning about Paris than I had been about London. This was because of the influence of N. I. Sedova. I was born and brought up in the country, but it was in Paris that I began to draw close to nature. And there, too, I came face to face with real art. I learned to appreciate painting, as well as nature, with great difficulty. One of Sedova s later entries says: "He expressed his general impression of Paris in this way: 'Resembles Odessa, but Odessa is better.' This absurd conclusion can be explained by the fact that L. D. was utterly absorbed in political life, and could see something else only when it forced itself upon him. He reacted to it as if it were a bother, something unavoidable. I did not agree with him in his estimate of Paris, and twitted him a little for this."

Yes, it was just like that. I was entering the atmosphere of a world centre with an obstinate and antagonistic attitude. At first, I "denied" Paris, and even tried to ignore it. Rightly considered, it was the case of a barbarian struggling for self-preservation. I felt that in order to get close to Paris and understand it fully, I would have to spend a great deal of mental energy. But I had my own world of revolution, and this was very exacting and brooked no rival interests. With difficulty, and by degrees, I was getting closer to art. I resisted the Louvre, the Luxembourg, and the exhibitions. Rubens seemed to me too well-fed and self-satisfied, Puvis de Chavannes too ascetic and faded, Carrière's portraits irritated me with their twilight ambiguousness. The same applied to sculpture and architecture. In point of fact, I was resisting art as I had resisted revolution earlier in life, and later, Marxism; as I had resisted, for several years, Lenin and his methods. The revolution of 1905 soon interrupted the progress of my communings with Europe and its culture. It was only during my second exile from Russia that I came closer to art—saw things, read, and even wrote a little about it. I never went beyond the stage of pure dilettantism, however.

In Paris, I heard Jaurès. It was at a time when Waldeck-Rousseau was at the head of the government, with Millerand as the minister of the Posts, and General Galliffet as the minister of war. I took part in a street demonstration of the Guesdists and shouted diligently, with the rest, all sorts of unpleasant things against Millerand. Jaurès did not make any great impression on me then. I felt too intensely that he was an enemy. Only several years later did I learn to appreciate that magnificent figure, even if my attitude toward Jaurèsism remained as hostile as before.

Pressed by the Marxist section of the students, Lenin agreed to give three lectures on the agrarian question at the Higher School organized in Paris by professors expelled from Russian universities. The liberal professors asked the undesirable lecturer to refrain from polemics as far as possible. But Lenin made no promise on this score, and began his first lecture with the statement that Marxism is a revolutionary theory, and therefore fundamentally polemical. I remember that Vladimir Ilyich was considerably excited before his first lecture, but as soon as he was on the platform he completely mastered himself, at least to all outward appearances. Professor Gambarov, who came to hear him speak, gave his impression to Deutsch in these words: "A perfect professor." He obviously thought this the highest praise.

Once we decided to take Lenin to the opera. All arrangements were intrusted to Sedova. Lenin went to the Opéra Comique with the same brief-case that accompanied him to his lectures. We sat in a group in the top gallery. Besides Lenin, Sedova, and myself, I believe the company included also Martov. An utterly unmusical reminiscence is always associated in my mind with this visit to the opera. In Paris Lenin had bought himself a pair of shoes that had turned out to be too tight. As fate would have it, I badly needed a new pair of shoes just then. I was given Lenin's, and at first I thought they fitted me perfectly. The trip to the opera was all right. But in the theatre I began to have pains. On the way home I suffered agonies, while Lenin twitted me all the more mercilessly because he had gone through the same thing for several hours in those very shoes.

From Paris, I went on a lecture tour of the Russian student colonies in Brussels, Liège, in Switzerland, and in some German towns. In Heidelberg, I listened to old Kuno Fischer, but I wasn't tempted by his Kantian teaching. The normative philosophy was foreign to my whole being. How could one prefer dry hay when next to it there was soft, juicy grass? Heidelberg had the name of being the centre of philosophical idealism among Russian students. One of their number was Avksentiev, the future minister of the Interior under the Kerensky government. I broke more than one lance there in my hot defense of materialist dialectics.

CHAPTER XII

THE PARTY CONGRESS AND THE SPLIT

WHEN Lenin went abroad at the age of thirty, he was already fully mature. In Russia, in the students' circles, in the Social Democratic groups, and in the exile colonies, he held first place. He could not fail to realize his power, if only because every one he met or worked with so clearly did. When he left Russia, he was already in possession of a full theoretical equipment and of a solid store of revolutionary experience. Abroad, there were collaborators waiting for him: "The Group of Liberation of Labor," and chief among them, Plekhanov, the brilliant Marxist interpreter, teacher of several generations, theorist, politician, publicist, and orator, with a European reputation and European connections. Side by side with Plekhanov were two other prominent authorities, Zasulitch and Axelrod. It was not only her heroic past that had placed Vera Zasulitch in the front ranks: she had an exceedingly sharp mind, an extensive background, chiefly historical, and a rare psychological insight. It was through Zasulitch that the "Group" in its day became connected with old Engels.

Unlike Plekhanov and Zasulitch, who were more closely bound to Latin socialism, Axelrod represented in the "Group" the ideas and experience of the German Social Democracy. In that period, however, Plekhanov was already beginning to enter upon a state of decline. His strength was being undermined by the very thing that was giving strength to Lenin— the approach of the revolution. All of Plekhanov's activity took place during the preparatory, theoretical days. He was Marxian propagandist and polemist-in-chief, but not a revolutionary politician of the proletariat. The nearer the shadow of the revolution crept, the more evident it became that Plekhanov was losing ground. He couldn't help seeing it himself, and that was the cause of his irritability toward the younger men.

The political leader of the *Iskra* was Lenin. Martov was the literary power; he wrote as easily and as continuously as he spoke. Working side by side with Lenin, Martov, his closest companion in arms, was already beginning to feel not quite at his ease. They were still addressing each other as "ty" (thou), but a certain coldness was beginning to creep into their mutual relations. Martov lived much more in the present, in its events, in his current literary work, in the political problems of the day, in the news and conversations; Lenin, on the other hand, although he was firmly intrenched in the present, was always trying to pierce the veil of the future. Martov evolved innumerable and often ingenious guesses, hypotheses, and propositions which even he promptly forgot; whereas Lenin waited until the moment when he needed them. The elaborate subtlety of Martov's ideas sometimes made Lenin shake his head in alarm. The different political lines had not yet had time to form; in fact, they had not even begun to make themselves felt. Later on, through the split at the Second Congress of the party, the *Iskra* adherents were divided into two groups, the "hard" and the "soft." These names were much in vogue at first. They indicated that, although no marked divisions really existed, there was a difference in point of view, in resoluteness and readiness to go on to the end.

One can say of Lenin and Martov that even before the split, even before the congress, Lenin was "hard" and Martov "soft." And they both knew it. Lenin would glance at Martov, whom he estimated highly, with a critical and somewhat suspicious look, and Martov, feeling his glance, would look down and move his thin shoulders nervously. When they met or conversed afterward, at least when I was present, one missed the friendly inflection and the jests. Lenin would look beyond Martov as he talked, while Martov's eyes would grow glassy under his drooping and never quite clean *pince-nez*. And when Lenin spoke to me of Martov, there was a peculiar intonation in his voice: "Who said that? Julius?"—and the name Julius was pronounced in a special way, with a slight emphasis, as if to give warning: "A good man, no question about it, even a remarkable one, but much too soft." At the same time, Martov was also coming under the influence of Vera Ivanovna Zasulitch, who was drawing him away from Lenin, not so much politically as psychologically.

Lenin concentrated all connections with Russia in his own hands. The secretary of the editorial board was his wife, Nadyezhda Konstantinovna Krupskaya. She was at the very centre of all the organization work; she received comrades when they arrived, instructed them when they left, established connections, supplied secret addresses, wrote letters, and coded and decoded correspondence. In her room there was always a smell of burned paper from the secret letters she heated over the fire to read. She often complained, in her gently insistent way, that people did not write enough, or that they got the code all mixed up, or wrote in chemical ink in such a way that one line covered another, and so forth.

Lenin was trying, in the every-day work of political organization, to achieve a maximum of independence from the older members and above all from Plekhanov, with whom he had had many bitter struggles, especially in the drafting of the party programme. Lenin's original draft, submitted as a counter-proposal to Plekhanov's, received from the latter a sharply unfavorable estimate, in the jesting and superior manner characteristic of Geórgy Valentinovitch on such occasions. But of course Lenin could not be confused or intimidated by such methods. The struggle took on a very dramatic aspect. Zasulitch and Martov acted as intermediaries; the former on behalf of Plekhanov, the latter of Lenin. Both intermediaries were in a most conciliatory mood, and besides this, they were friends. Vera Ivanovna, according to her own account, once said to Lenin: "George [Plekhanov] is a hound—he will shake a thing for a while, and then drop it; whereas you are a bulldog—yours is the death-grip." When she repeated this conversation to me later, Vera Ivanovna added: "This appealed to Lenin very much—'a death-grip,' he repeated, with obvious delight." As she said this, she good-naturedly mimicked Lenin's intonation and accent. (He could not pronounce the sound of "r" clearly.)

All these disagreements took place before I arrived from Russia. I never suspected them. Nor did I know that the relations among the editors of the *Iskra* had been aggravated even more by my coming. Four months after my arrival, Lenin wrote to Plekhanov:

"March 2, 1903. PARIS.

"I suggest to all the members of the editorial board that they co-optate 'Pero' as a member of the board on the same basis as other members. I believe co-optation demands not merely a majority of votes, but a unanimous decision. We *very much need* a seventh member, both as a convenience in voting (six being an even number), and as an addition to our forces. 'Pero' has been contributing to every issue for several months now; he works in general most energetically for the *Iskra;* he gives lectures (in which he has been very successful). In the section of articles and notes on the events of the day, he will not only be very useful, but absolutely necessary. Unquestionably a man of rare abilities, he has conviction and energy, and he will go much farther. Furthermore, in the field of translations and of popular literature, he will be able to do a great deal. Possible objections: (1) His youth; (2) his leaving for Russia, possibly in a short time; (3) his pen [pero], this time without the quotation, which shows traces of the feuilleton style, and is excessively florid, etc.

"Re (1) 'Pero' is proposed not for any independent post, but only as a member of the board. There he will acquire his experience. He has unquestionably the 'sense' of a party man, of a man of faction, and knowledge and experience are a matter of time. The co-optation is necessary in order to tie him down and encourage him.

"Re (2) If 'Pero' does enter into an intimate contact with all of our work, he will probably not leave so early. If he does leave, his organized connection with the board and his working under its instruction will not constitute a minus, but an enormous plus.

"Re (3) The defects of style are not a matter of importance. He will outgrow them. At present, he accepts 'corrections' in silence (and not very readily). On the board there will be discussions, votings, and the 'instructions' will have a more definite and obligatory character.

"To sum up, I propose: (1) to pass a vote by all the six members of the board for a full co-optation of 'Pero'; (2) to start, if he is accepted, on the definite formulation of the relations among the editors, of the rules of voting, and on the drafting of a precise constitution. *This is necessary for ourselves,* as well as for the congress.

"P.S. I consider that it would be *very inconvenient* and awkward *to put off* the co-optation, as it has been made clear to me that 'Pero' is *considerably* annoyed—though of course he does not show it openly—about his being still up in the air, and about his being treated, as it seems to him, as a 'youth.' If we do not accept 'Pero' at once, and he goes away, say, a month from now, to Russia, I am convinced that he will interpret this as our *direct unwillingness* to accept him on the board. He will slip away and this will be very undesirable."

I quote this letter, which I discovered only recently, almost in its entirety (excepting only technical details) because it is extremely characteristic of the situation within the editorial board, characteristic of Lenin himself, and of his attitude toward me. As I have already said, I was completely ignorant of the struggle that was going on behind the scenes with regard to my joining the board. Lenin's idea that I was "considerably annoyed" about my not being included on the board is incorrect and not in the least characteristic of my mood at that time. In point of fact, it never entered my mind. My attitude toward the board was that of a pupil toward his masters. I was only twenty-three years old. The youngest of the editors was Martov, who was seven years older than I, and Lenin himself was ten years my senior. I was much pleased with the fate that had placed me so close to this remarkable group of people. I could learn much from each of them, and I did, most diligently.

Where did Lenin get the idea that I was annoyed? I think it was simply a tactical trick. The entire letter is imbued with the desire to prove, to convince, and to get what he wanted. Lenin purposely tried to scare the other editors with my supposed annoyance and possible estrangement from the *Iskra*. He used this merely as an additional argument, and nothing more. The same also applies to his argument about my being referred to as a "youth." This was the name by which old Deutsch frequently addressed me, but no one else did. And to Deutsch, who never had and never could have any political influence over me, I was only bound by genuine friendship. Lenin used the argument merely to impress on the older ones the necessity of reckoning with me, as with a man who was politically mature.

Ten days after Lenin's letter had been sent, Martov wrote to Axelrod:

"March 10, 1903. LONDON.

"Vladimir Ilyich has proposed to us that we admit 'Pero,' whom you know, to the board of editors, with full rights. His literary work shows undeniable talent, he is quite 'ours' in thought, he has wholly identified himself with the interests of the *Iskra,* and here, abroad, he wields considerable influence, thanks to his exceptional eloquence. He speaks magnificently; he could not do better. Of this, both Vladimir Ilyich and I have had occasion to convince ourselves. He has knowledge and works hard to increase it. I unreservedly subscribe to Vladimir Ilyich's proposal."

In this letter, Martov shows himself only as a true echo of Lenin. But he does not repeat the argument about my annoyance. I lived with Martov, side by side in the same house. He had observed me too closely to suspect any impatient desire on my part to become a member of the board.

Why did Lenin insist so eagerly on the necessity of my joining the board? He wanted to obtain a stable majority. On a number of important questions, the editors were divided into two equal groups: the older ones (Plekhanov, Zasulitch, Axelrod), and the younger generation (Lenin, Martov, Potresov). Lenin felt sure that on the most critical questions I would be with him. On one occasion, when it was necessary to oppose Plekhanov, Lenin called me aside and said slyly: "Let Martov speak. He will smooth it over, whereas you will hit straight from the shoulder." Observing an expression of surprise on my face, he added immediately: "For my part, I prefer to hit from the shoulder, but with Plekhanov it would be better this time to smooth things over."

Lenin's proposal that I be put on the board was wrecked by Plekhanov's opposition. Worse still, this proposal became the chief cause of an extremely unfriendly attitude on Plekhanov's part toward me, because he guessed that Lenin was looking for a firm majority against him. The question of reorganizing the editorial board was deferred until the congress. The board decided, however, without waiting for the congress, to invite me to the editorial meetings in an advisory capacity. Plekhanov resolutely opposed even this. But Vera Ivanovna said to him, "I'll bring him, no matter what you say." And she did actually "bring" me to the next meeting. As I knew nothing about what had happened behind the scenes, I was much put out by the studied coldness with which Geórgy Valentinovitch shook hands with me, a thing at which he was past-master. Plekhanov's dislike of me lasted for a long time; in fact, it never disappeared. In April, 1904, Martov, in writing to Axelrod, referred to "his [Plekhanov's] personal hatred of the said person [myself]—a hatred that is degrading to himself and ignoble."

The reference in Lenin's letter to my literary style at that time is interesting. It is true in both respects, that is, regarding my tendency to florid writing, and also my disinclination to accept corrections. My writing was an affair of only about two years' standing at that time, and the question of style held an important and independent place with me. I was just beginning to appreciate the flavor of words. Just as children rub their gums when they are teething, sometimes with quite inappropriate objects, I would pursue words, formulas, or an image in my literary teething-stage. Only time would purify my style. And as the struggle for form was neither an accidental nor an external thing, but a reflection of my intellectual processes, it is no wonder that, with all my respect for editors, I instinctively protected my still shaping individuality as a writer against the inroads of men who were already mature but differently constituted.

Meanwhile, the day set for the congress was drawing near, and eventually it was decided to transfer the editorial board to Geneva, in Switzerland, where living was cheaper and contact with Russia easier. Lenin agreed to this with a heavy heart. "In Geneva, we were put up in two tiny attic rooms," writes Sedova. "L. D. was engrossed in the work for the congress, while I was getting ready to leave for party work in Russia." The first delegates to the congress began to arrive, and there were continuous conferences. In this preparatory work, the leadership unquestionably belonged to Lenin, although the fact was not always obvious. Some delegates arrived with doubts or with pretensions. The work of preparation took a great deal of time. Much time was given to the consideration of the proposed constitution, since one of the important points in the scheme of organization was the relationship to be established